Thee & Me

A Beginner's Guide to Early Quaker Records

Thee & Me

A Beginner's Guide to Early Quaker Records

Lisa Parry Arnold

Dedication

I dedicate this book to the Lord

who loved, delighted in, and led

the Quakers

as He does you

as He does me.

Table of Contents

Table of Contents
Detailed View

Table of Contents

The early Quakers used terms and phrases that are often confusing to researchers. This chapter explains their unique vernacular in an effort to assist you in navigating through the records.

Early Quakers were encouraged to record information about the families and individuals in their congregations. As a result, they often captured more details than even the Church of England parish registers. These practices continued when they immigrated, so member records beginning in about 1662 (nearly 200 years prior to the collecting of state vital records) contain the kind of detail that researchers always hope to find about their ancestors. This chapter examines each record type and what to expect to find in them.

Certificates of Removal (removal is an English term meaning "to relocate") are often essential sources of information for research. The process of moving from meeting to meeting provided documents that can help to track the migration of Quaker ancestors. However, few records cause researchers as much confusion as the disciplinary actions of Quaker meetings. This chapter outlines the concepts behind both of these record types and how they affect research.

You may have heard of a collection called "Hinshaw" or the "Encyclopedia of American Quaker Genealogy." You may have even tried to use this resource to locate your Quaker ancestor and ended up confused by the abbreviations. This chapter discusses the Hinshaw collections, both the published and unpublished, and gives researchers important clues concerning this large body of work including the abbreviations created especially for each volume.

When you begin researching Quaker records, you may find, as others have, that the way Quakers dated their letters, minutes, and other documents can be a bit confusing. You may even be tempted to "correct" the dates that you find when you record the information. This chapter examines the reasoning behind the Quaker calendar and dating practices of 300 years ago and how it applies to your research today.

This chapter focuses on some excellent resources that are currently available to Quaker researchers. It includes a discussion about online resources that provide new tools and lists physical repositories that offer finding aids (books and articles) about specific Quaker meetings.

This chapter explores the reasoning behind some unique Quaker practices such as: plain clothes, Plain language, and swearing of oaths. Learning about Quaker ancestors does not include just their names; it also begs an understanding of their lives and insight into their most common practices. Not every member followed the practices outlined here, but most Quakers felt it was part of their Christian faith to do so.

Quaker meeting houses are still standing in towns and cities throughout the eastern and mid-western United States. They are distinct in style and appearance, and they serve as charming reminders of years long ago. Burial grounds were often part of the property and were not restricted to members only. In fact, anyone was permitted to be buried there, including slaves and American Indians. This chapter will give you a better understanding of meeting houses, funerals, and the unusual headstones used in Quaker burial grounds.

This chapter focuses on some of the essentials of genealogical research, such as: considerations when hiring a professional to help with research, annual genealogy conferences and seminars, and Quaker-related societies.

This chapter presents a small research project and analysis, using three of the databases in the Quaker Collection on Ancestry.com:

1. *Hinshaw Index to Selected Quaker Records, 1680–1940*
2. *North America, Quaker Monthly Meetings Index, 1671–2010*
3. *U.S., Quaker Meeting Records, 1681–1994*

The *Hinshaw Index to Selected Quaker Records, 1680-1940* is an excellent resource for Quaker researchers, especially when they gain a level of comfort in using them. Together we will research one family, using both the Hinshaw Index (number one on the list above) and original Quaker Meeting records (number three on the list above), while we attempt to construct the context of their lives in a given time period.

Preface

WRITING THIS BOOK IS THE fulfillment of a promise for me, a promise I made in a dream.

You could say it is in my blood. I was raised as a Quaker in the Philadelphia area, a 10th generation descendant of Quakers on 9 of my 16 family lines. I was a birthright member of Westfield Friends Meeting in Cinnaminson, Burlington County, New Jersey, which is the same meeting that my family had attended since 1816. My parents were active members and served on various committees; and I attended the Philadelphia Yearly Meeting for many years as the youth delegate. During my high school years, I attended George School (class of 1971), a Quaker boarding school in Bucks County, Pennsylvania, where my parents and grandparents met as students.

While growing up, I heard many stories of the early Quakers. I was blessed to know my grandparents and others of their generation, whom I revere and strive to honor in my work. My grandfather told me about his much-beloved first cousin, Alice Paul, an American Suffragist and women's rights activist, who wrote the original Equal Rights Amendment in 1923. My mother told me of her third great-grandfather, the courageous

FIGURE P-1: *Alice Stokes Paul, suffragist and women's rights activist, 1885-1977. Alice Paul was born to a Quaker family that believed in gender equality, education for women, and working to improve society.*

Isaac Potts, who gave his home to George Washington during the long, snowy winter of 1777 in Valley Forge, PA, even while knowing that to support the war effort in any way could have been grounds for disownment from the Quakers.

As a child, I knew that my Quaker heritage was special, and had family lines extending back to the early church leaders and Colonial governors. I later became the happy recipient of the family research performed by a cousin, Beulah Haines Parry, who shared her love of family history with my mother and aunts, who, in turn, shared it with me. Cousin Beulah captured the old stories on large charts in the 1940s and 1950s, carefully citing each source, including book titles and page numbers. I was thrilled to continue her research. But, it wasn't until I had the dream that the influence of my Quaker heritage made its greatest impact on me.

This dream came to me several years ago. In it, a large group of Quaker men and women dressed in 17th- century clothes asked if I would help their descendants find them. I don't remember many of my dreams, but this one was quite vivid and has remained with me in great detail. I made a solemn promise to help the Quakers, who visited me that night, but I had no idea what kind of "help" I could provide—after all, I was only one person!

In 2001, after raising my family, I returned to college. As I began my studies in Family History at Brigham Young University, I learned that the resources for Quaker researchers were fairly limited and quite dated. The records for the early Quakers were safely preserved in college libraries, which required Quaker researchers to travel in order to use them for research. In addition, the most recent research guide had been published in the 1980s. I wasn't sure where my journey would lead me, but in the senior year of my studies, I applied for and was granted an internship at Swarthmore College. My fourth great-grandfather was instrumental in founding Swarthmore and many of my family members attended the school, so it seemed a likely place to familiarize myself with the records. The time that I spent at the Swarthmore Friends Historical Library enabled me to learn about and work with 300-year-old Quaker records in the largest collection in the United States. I combined my research with reading many books written by and about early Quakers and their history. But even after I completed the internship, I had no idea how it might lead me toward helping descendants find their Quaker ancestors. I thought that perhaps I should stay near Swarthmore and help clients with their Quaker research. Then everything changed.

Ancestry.com hired me and I began work on the Content Acquisition team, specializing in the acquisition of church records. Quite soon thereafter, a consortium of Quaker colleges approached Ancestry.com to see if we were interested in acquiring their collections of Quaker records. That day nearly five years ago, launched my involvement in a landmark Quaker records project. Plans to bring the massive Quaker record collection online started to unfold, plans that would revolutionize the way Quaker research was performed. Microfilm reels and books by the hundreds were scanned and digitized. All of the Quaker names that appeared in the records were extracted and keyed, making them more easily searchable. The names dated from the late 1500s in England to the early 1900s in the United States; from England and Wales to Pennsylvania, Virginia and Maryland; from the Southern states through the Midwest to Iowa and Nebraska.

My involvement expanded beyond Content Acquisition over the course of the project, when various teams working on the records at Ancestry.com requested lectures in which I acquainted them with the history of the Quakers; they could sense the uniqueness of the records they were handling. I also started giving lectures at genealogy conferences to groups of descendants of early Quakers, each of whom desired more information and a deeper connection to their heritage. All the while, the monumental task of scanning, digitizing, extracting, and keying the colleges' Quaker collections continued. It took several years and an enormous company-wide effort to complete this project, but the date was finally announced when the Quaker records would appear online at Ancestry.com. Despite this wonderful news, there was one thing missing: a guide to the records.

What was needed was an easily readable guide that would educate new researchers about both the history of the Quakers and the idiosyncrasies of the records, including how to do research within online collections. Although I had compiled a book from the notes I took while completing my internship at Swarthmore College, I didn't see myself as qualified enough to write such a book. Eventually, however, I realized that over the years I had been blessed with both the heritage and the experiences to do just that. I decided that the book would speak not only about the records but also about the people. Early Quaker leaders had deeply inspired me when I learned about the sacrifices they made in order to live according to the dictates of their consciences. I wanted other descendants to know about the suffering of the early Quakers at the hands of the British government, which sent thousands to prison or sold them into slavery for "crimes" such as, refusing to pay tithes to the Anglican Church and speaking in public about their religion. I felt it was important to highlight the sometimes charming, sometimes unpleasant details that were recorded in monthly business meetings by faithful clerks since the 1600s. I have anguished with those who wrote of the heartbreak they experienced during the Separation of 1827, an event that divided the Quakers into two separate bodies in most every Meeting, and I knew that other descendants would feel the same anguish. I have reveled in the work of Tom Hill, who labored for years assembling details about every Quaker meeting in North America and placed it freely online, just to help others. Because of the relative obscurity of these early historical facts, I thought that other descendants might not be aware of them or know of Hill's website and other new tools that are extremely useful for Quaker research. I wanted to write a book with enough basic instruction and insights to help descendants start their research and to point them toward other resources, should they want to learn more. With the help of my loving family, friends, and co-workers, the book has finally arrived.

So, now you know why I wrote, "Thee & Me: A Beginner's Guide to Early Quaker Records". It is the culmination of a journey for me, a journey that started with an unforgettable dream. I trust that you will find the contents to be of value as you research your early Quaker ancestors. I sincerely hope that, with the help of this guide, you will learn enough about your ancestors to be able to greet them with a knowing smile, should they ever find their way into *your* dreams.

Lisa
April 2014

Acknowledgements

I WOULD FIRST LIKE TO thank the early Quakers, especially my ancestors, who have been endlessly inspiring to me. Following closely behind are the authors of numerous histories of the early Quakers; their works helped me to feel a deeper connection to my past, and shaped my understanding through their words.

I would like to express my gratitude to the many people who encouraged the writing of this book and to all those who supported, talked about, and willingly reviewed its many drafts. Your ideas and comments were essential, and have improved it immensely. I am also indebted to those who assisted in the copyediting, proofreading and design.

A big thank you goes to the knowledgeable staff at Swarthmore Friends Historical Library who taught me the essentials of Quaker research. To my bosses at Ancestry.com, along with the entire Content Acquisition Team, you have been extremely supportive and more than helpful in directing my paths. Lastly, my most heartfelt thanks go to my family who managed both the project and the author with immense talent, finesse and a whole lot of love and forbearance.

I am solely responsible for any inaccuracies contained in this book.

Introduction

THIS BOOK IS DESIGNED TO help researchers to understand more about their early Quaker ancestors and covers the first 200 years of their existence. The early Quakers had a unique way of speaking, of dressing, of doing business. Their church structure was unlike any other religion, before or after. They refused to take up arms, against anyone, for any reason. They believed that men and women are equal, and that all races and nationalities are equal as God's children. They believed that everyone should be educated and thus welcomed all children to their schools, in a time when the children of slaves and American Indians and even female children were excluded from most schools.

You may find, as you explore the records of the past, that some of these curious facts appear:

- In various documents, your ancestor "affirms" rather than "swears" that a fact is true.

- Your ancestor counts his months and days in numbers like 4th month and 14th day.

- The word "Friend," capitalized, appears in an ancestor's will.

This book will help you discover the reasons behind these peculiarities!

You will not only learn about the kinds of records they kept, but it is my hope that you will gain an understanding and appreciation for these honored ancestors. Although the early Quakers lived over 300 years ago, by reading their meeting minutes, we can learn much about the difficulties they faced and their successful pattern for living lives of personal restraint and quiet testimony. Their choices are often misinterpreted by modern generations, but their decisions were mostly guided by love—love of their family and friends, their religious convictions, the scriptures, and the Lord. They were Christians of the highest devotion.

Introduction

This quote from the *Guide to the Records of Philadelphia Yearly Meeting* explains the significance of the Quaker records and why I revere and admire my Quaker ancestors:

"Quaker Meeting records illustrate the beliefs and practices of a religious community, the Society of Friends, which formed in England in the 1650s and endured through a common pattern of 'silent' worship. In the service for worship, men and women gathered to share their experiences of the Inward Light and to seek guidance in their search for a spiritually sensitive and ethically demanding pattern of life. Friends remained an influential people who shared in governing Pennsylvania until the Revolution. They pioneered the Native American rights movement after 1755, created the anti-slavery crusade, and played significant roles in the temperance and women's rights movements."

Quaker family history research can be a rewarding adventure. For three centuries, the Quaker records have been carefully preserved and protected against the ravages of time in a few locations in the United States and England. And now, thanks to Ancestry.com, it is the perfect time to do research in the Quaker records. With records available online and indexed, it is easier than ever to be successful in finding your Quaker ancestors and adding them to your family tree.

People are interested in learning about their family roots for various reasons. Some have seen the popular television program *Who Do You Think You Are?* and want to have a similar experience. Some just want to know how their ancestors lived several centuries ago. Others want to generate interest for the next generation, hoping that they will have a deeper appreciation for their heritage. I became interested many decades ago when my aunts and mother would tell me about my Quaker ancestors. I was born into the Quaker religion, the 10th generation of Quakers, on most of my family lines. I attended a Quaker boarding school (George School in Bucks County, PA, where my siblings, parents, and grandparents also attended), and I was married in a Quaker wedding. Now, I want to share this legacy with my children and grandchildren, so that they might have the same pride in their Quaker heritage.

I think you will find, as I have found, that being a descendant of the early Quakers is a very special privilege. As you read through the records, you will see that they were a determined, thrifty, courageous, hard-working, and above all, Christian people. They were adept at business, philanthropic with their means, skilled at political leadership, and fair-minded to their non-Quaker neighbors of all races and religions. Very early in the establishment of the colony, they built not only homes and church buildings, but also trade schools, colleges, hospitals, parks, museums, and banks, all of which thrived in their day and many of which are still in existence. Their work with the American Indians, the slaves (Underground Railroad), and women's rights (my Quaker cousin, Alice Paul, wrote the original Equal Rights Amendment) helped to establish new and significant changes, both politically and socially.

Finding your Quaker ancestors is a rewarding experience. I look forward to helping you in your journey of discovery. If you want to contact me and share your journey, I would enjoy hearing from you. Please email me at Lisa@quakerancestors.com.

A few important reminders:

• Not *all* Quakers did the same things, individually or as congregations. There were no set rules to cover every situation, just general guidelines. While most congregations operated in a similar manner, changes occurred as time passed, as people moved to the frontier, and as generations got further away from the early Friends.

• Many names from this time period are similar, so carefully determine which one is your ancestor—a vital first step to keep you from climbing *someone else's* family tree.

Let's begin!

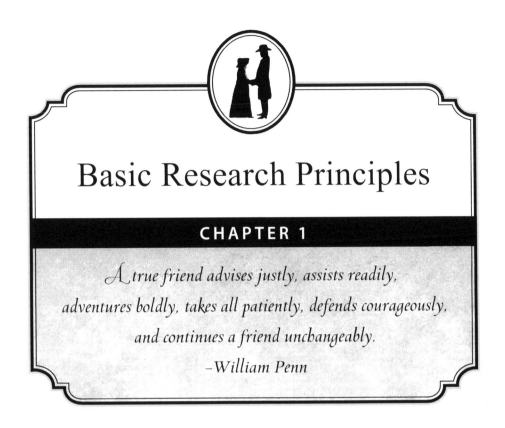

Basic Research Principles

CHAPTER 1

A true friend advises justly, assists readily, adventures boldly, takes all patiently, defends courageously, and continues a friend unchangeably.
–William Penn

THIS CHAPTER OUTLINES PRINCIPLES FOR successful genealogical research, including Quaker research. You can focus your research by following a few simple guidelines that have been discovered by others who started their journeys before you. You will find that if you are willing to read through this chapter before jumping into the records on Ancestry.com or building a family tree online, you will be able to avoid many of the pitfalls and headaches that come from making uninformed errors.

Family history can be challenging, for no sooner do you uncover the record of one ancestor than the records of other family members emerge and you become fascinated with another era. You speak with older members of the family and their eyes moisten as they speak of family gatherings and family stories. You begin to wonder which stories are fact and which ones are fiction and start to log the events, dates, and people being discussed, maybe even creating a timeline. And then, you find you are hooked and your life becomes enriched in ways you never imagined.

Begin with What You Know

When doing family history research, always begin with what you know and move backward in time to create a solid foundation first. There are enough records available now, both online and in libraries, to corroborate (or not) the stories you have heard your elder family members share. So, start with the

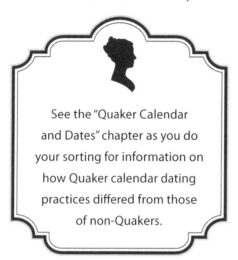

See the "Quaker Calendar and Dates" chapter as you do your sorting for information on how Quaker calendar dating practices differed from those of non-Quakers.

current generation before moving to the previous one. Ask family members for copies of records they have; ask for time to interview them; search for memorabilia and family documents anywhere you can find them—in trunks, in attics, in closets. Among other documents, you may find old letters, photographs, birth certificates, christening records, newspaper clippings, prayer cards, scrapbooks, wedding invitations, military service papers, and other wonderful family mementos that will help you put the puzzle pieces together. Sort them according to family groupings and inventory what you find. Then place them in chronological order.

Interview Older Family Members

Ask for time with older family members during family visits and holidays. It is much easier for them to recall events if you are there asking them questions in person rather than via email. Your questions and reactions to their stories will often stir more memories and bring out previously untold events that you will cherish. One way to preserve these memories is to set up a video camera or voice recorder somewhere in the room where it will not inhibit the speaker. This way, you can record the speaker and then type up the memories later. This way you are free to simply listen and react to the wealth of knowledge shared during the interview. Write down all of the names, dates, and places that are mentioned in the recording. Family folklore, *while not always accurate*, can hold wonderful clues. Capture it all for now, then later when you get into the records, you can separate fact from family legend.

Gain an Understanding of the History Your Ancestors Lived Through

Take the time to learn about the historical events that took place where your ancestors lived, and your research will begin to "come alive" for you! Knowing that there was a flood in a particular region, or a flu epidemic, or a war or other political upheaval, will cause you to consider the impact of that event on the family you are researching. Were they there? Were they affected? Could that be why so many members of the family died within a few weeks of each other? Or why groups moved en masse to a new place?

You may want to review the *Quaker Events Worth Noting* in Chapter Three, which will give you an idea of where Quakers were living and migrating, generally speaking. As you become familiar with the historical events in the lives of the Quakers, you will develop a better sense of the life of your ancestor. The more you study the local history and culture, the more you may begin to understand some of the reasons behind the decisions they made.

Share Your Research

Create an online family tree at Ancestry.com and invite your cousins and other extended family members to view it and add to what you have posted. Your pedigree chart will grow much more quickly with collaboration from multiple family members. Other family members may have scanned photos and documents and attached them to their tree. I encourage you to check them out; I have found photos this way that I had never seen before. If you see that someone you don't know has added information from your online tree to theirs, click on their username and send a note. Such communications are anonymous (brokered through Ancestry.com) until you decide to reveal your own email address and communicate more easily. You might find several cousins this way! The age of the Internet is a wonderful time to do family history for this reason.

To search the Ancestry.com collection of Family Histories, Journals & Biographies and look for books written about your Quaker ancestors, click on the Search tab at the top of the home page. Enter the surname in the Last Name box and add the state in the Location box. At the bottom of the search box, you can scroll down to check (or uncheck) any of the collections. To search for a family history, uncheck all but "Stories & publications," and be sure that the Collection Priority is set to "United States."

Has Anyone Written About Your Family Before?

Sometimes, you have the good fortune of finding a book that was written about one of your family lines. Many of the early Quaker families have been written about by current generations. These books will have dates, names, and places that will help to fill out your family tree. There are several places to look for family histories - Ancestry.com has tens of thousands of unpublished family histories, as does the Family History Library in Salt Lake City. Swarthmore Friends Historical Library in Swarthmore, PA, also has family histories in addition to its Family and Personal Papers collection.

To search the catalog for the holdings at the Family History Library, go to FamilySearch.org and click on Search at the top of the page. Clicking on Catalog at the top of the next page takes you to the FamilySearch Catalog page. Here, click on Surnames under "Search by:" and a Surnames field opens. Type the surname that you are researching into the Surnames field and click the Search button. The results page includes a list of titles containing that surname.

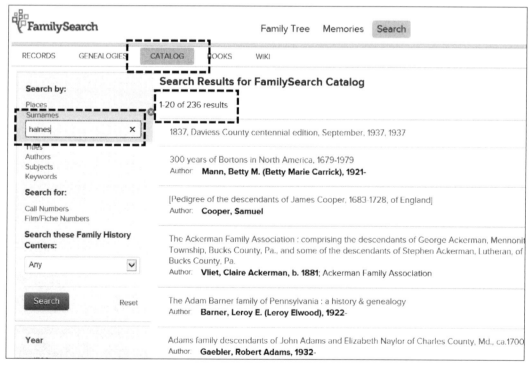

FIGURE 1-1: FamilySearch has the world's largest collection of family histories. They are scanning them to make them accessible online.

Location Search
Has Anyone Written About the Town or County You Are Researching?

Did you know that each community in the United States was encouraged to write a local history around the time of the centennial celebration of our country (1876)? They were asked to include the details about the establishment of the community, short biographies of prominent members, church and school histories, and other highlights. Many of the early Quakers are described in these local or county histories. The challenge is finding them. There are several places to look:

1. Ancestry.com has a huge local history collection. To access it, go to the home page, and just hover the pointer over the Search tab. A drop-down menu appears. Click on Card Catalog. On the Card Catalog page, enter the town or county that you are searching into the Keyword(s) field. Click the Search button. A list of titles pertaining to that area should appear. For example, a search for Bucks County, PA produces a list of 69 titles of books and collections. You can sort the results by various parameters using the Sort By drop-down menu in the upper right corner

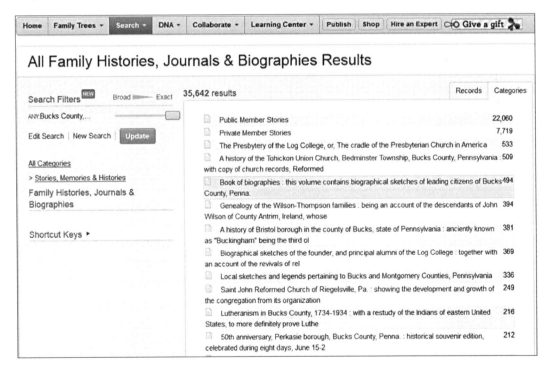

FIGURE 1-2: Showing some of the titles from the extensive collection of family and local histories on Ancestry.com.

2. The Periodical Source Index (PERSI, created by the ACPL) is a PERiodocal Source Index. It is accessible through Heritage Quest at most local libraries. PERSI is a list of published articles written about different places and surnames that were indexed by the ACPL. When you click on PERSI, you will see a drop box where you can select your search preference; you can search by Surname, US Locality, Canada, Foreign Locality, or Methodology. When you find that someone has written about the subject, location, or name you are searching for, PERSI will give you a list of repositories that stock that magazine.

EXAMPLE: When selecting Land Records in Burlington County, NJ, you will see a list of ten articles and societies with information. When you click on each link, you will see a list of publishers as well as the address of the Allen County Public Library, which hosts PERSI. The staff at ACPL is willing to look up information and send copies of articles, which can be a real time and money saver. PERSI a great resource that will lead you to a wealth of materials. Many people don't know about it; you might want to check it out!

FIGURE 1-3: "The PERSI Archive" is a valuable resource when researching articles written about ancestors & their locales. "HeritageQuest Online" can be accessed through your local library.

3. The largest repository for local histories is the Family History Library in Salt Lake City. Search the catalog by going to FamilySearch.org and clicking Search at the top of the page. The Discover Your Family History page opens. To research a particular location, complete the Country field and the State or Province field, then click the Search button. The next page shows a list of results; click the Records and Collections tabs at the top to see which format you prefer. If the books on the results page have been "filmed" (converted to microfilm), you can order those films from your local The Church of Jesus Christ of Latter-day Saints (LDS) Family History Center. But, you might get lucky and be able to read it online! Thousands of published family histories, city and county histories, historic city directories, and related records are being scanned in order to be available on the Internet. The books being converted to digital formats are from the Allen County Public Library, Brigham Young University's various libraries, the Family History Library in Salt Lake City, the Clayton Library Center for Genealogical Research in Houston, and the Midwest Genealogy Center at the Mid-Continent Public Library in Independence, Missouri. Together they are building the world's most comprehensive collection of family, and city and county histories.

Local Historical Societies

The Quaker researcher has a special advantage in that there are excellent local historical and genealogical societies in the counties where most of the early Quakers settled. Conferring with the experts in those societies, reading copies of their quarterly publications, and becoming familiar with their collections is also a great way to get started. You may even want to consider joining their societies. The annual membership fees are generally quite reasonable and are collected to support their efforts, enabling you to use their websites and collections. Researchers who join the genealogy or historical society in each of the counties where their ancestors lived often find valuable information through the members who live and work with the records from those counties.

The Value of Keeping a Research Log

A research log (see blank sample) is a highly recommended way to track your progress. It is a visible reflection of the work you have accomplished and an easy way to plan for the future. Many people who are trying to find their ancestors use research logs and other such documents to track these types of information:

- comments made by relatives about individuals and families

- resources to check in various repositories during subsequent visits

- which resources they have searched, the parameters they used, and the positive and negative results of their research; especially important if the researcher wants to revisit those resources

- books or online collections that they hear about and want to pursue when they get a chance

Research logs are a valuable tracking device as well as a project plan. If you create one log for each family, it is easier to keep the information pertinent. One suggested method is to maintain your research log electronically, such as on a laptop. This way, it becomes a dynamic log, ever growing and changing. But it also provides a bread-crumb trail so that you can go back to any resource, because you know where you looked, on what day, what name you were searching for, and what you found, even if you found nothing at the time. Sometimes, as you learn more about the person that you are researching (and more about the record that you are examining), you realize that you missed something the first time around. In those instances, you will be very glad that you took the time to write down the information for that resource (book and page, or website) so that you can easily go right back to it and double-check your former findings.

Plan to create a folder or file for each family, by surname, and you will find that you can keep the documents relating to each family in one place. It is a good idea to keep a folder for each family on your computer for digital files and images, and a physical folder at home for printed copies. You may find that by getting out the magnifying glass and re-examining the paper copies, information that you skipped over on previous readings becomes apparent. It is also helpful to revisit the documents in these folders as your family history research expands, because historical documents often make more sense or can even take on new meaning as the pieces of the genealogical puzzle fall into place.

				Page Sheet of

Research Record Sheet

Surname:_____ Researcher:_____ Date: _____
Locality: _____ Address: _____

Entry Date	Repository Call No.	Indexed Condition	Description of Source (Sufficient for Citation)	Purpose Name, period, etc.	Comments	Doc. No.
1						
2						
3						
4						
5						
6						
7						
8						

Check if continued on other side ☐

FIGURE 1-4: Use Research logs as a valuable tracking device as well as for creating a project plan.

In Summary

The joy in discovering your ancestors is wonderfully infectious. Somehow, knowing that one's ancestors endured difficult times and faced challenging decisions yet managed to keep their families together and prosper against all odds, can be a source of strength for today's researchers. Enjoy your personal journey but also find a way to share it with your family members. Studies have shown that children and youth are strengthened by the stories of their ancestors and tend to make better life decisions when they know the stories of their family's history.

Basic Quaker History and Key Leaders

CHAPTER 2

If we will not be governed by God,
we will be governed by tyrants.
–William Penn

THIS CHAPTER FOCUSES ON THE origin of the Quaker religion. A brief education on the religious turmoil during the English Reformation Period and the heavy persecution against the Society of Friends, as well as other nonconformist groups, will help you understand some of their decisions. This chapter examines some of the issues Quakers faced and the courage and faith that kept them going in spite of heavy persecution.

During the reign of the Stuarts in the early 1600s, there was a general unrest from the people in England concerning religion. The Puritans expressed their frustration with the throne, and the Church of England did all it could to crush them. Groups with similarly radical ideas included: the Seekers, the Separatists, the Presbyterians, the Independents, the Parliamentarians, the Royalists, the High Churchmen, and the Nonconformists. The Civil War in England (1642–1651) incited a season of political, social, and religious passion. Quakers were strongly opposed to oppression brought about by the Church of England but also spoke out about the Roman Catholic Church. It was a protest against war, against slavery, and against cruelty of any man against another, often done in the name of religion. It was into this arena that George Fox stepped.

George Fox

George Fox was born in 1624 to a humble, religious home. The son of a weaver, Fox left home in his early 20s searching for answers to the hypocrisy that he saw in the organized religions of his day. He called himself a "troubled soul in search of rest." During his journey, he sought answers from several priests, but he eventually found his answers in the New Testament of the King James Bible. The Bible had been available only to members of the clergy until the 1640s, when it was finally printed and distributed across England in a format and size that was available to the common man. In his journal, Fox indicates that when he had exhausted all possible

GEORGE FOX.

FIGURE 2-1: George Fox is considered to be the founder of the Quaker faith.

sources for help and felt himself failing in his faith, he heard a voice that said, "There is one, even Christ Jesus that can speak to thy condition". He then records, "and when I heard it, my heart did leap for joy."

Fox based an entire religion on two primary concepts, the first being that only the Lord can offer redemption—it cannot come from any man or religious movement. The second concept was that men and women could receive direct divine revelation for their lives and that guidance is more important to their lives than anything else. He encouraged his followers to "wait upon the Lord." Their worship services therefore became an hour or more of sitting together and worshipping in silence as they each "waited upon the Lord." He based this worship method on the Biblical scripture in Matthew 18:20, "For where two or three have gathered together in my name, there am I in the midst of them." It is not difficult to imagine that this new religion, which encouraged a focus on one's personal relationship with God, caused a major disturbance among the priests from both the Church of England and the Roman Catholic Church.

The New Religion Quickly Becomes Popular

As news of his concepts spread, Fox gained supporters from many levels of English society and from many age groups. The English Reformation had spread across the land, and people were ready for a new, more open, more "just" religion such as this one—one that did not discriminate on the basis of wealth or societal position and was open to people of all backgrounds and stations. By the mid-1600s, people began to speak openly about their convictions. Families read the Bible in the evenings with enthusiasm, looking for answers to life's questions, no longer feeling the need to confine their beliefs to those of Catholicism or the Church of England. When the Quakers decided to stop paying tithes, though, the disturbance became uproar. Many Quakers were imprisoned and their homes confiscated by the king in an attempt to quash this bold new religion. The persecutions of the Quakers went on for years with no relief in sight. In fact, Parliament passed the Conventicle Act in 1664, banning all non-Anglican meetings for religious worship where more than five people were present. So, essentially, only Church of England meetings could be held, and it became legal to arrest people attending any other meetings.

Fox continued preaching throughout England and eventually traveled to Ireland, Germany, Holland, Barbados, Jamaica, and the American colonies. As a result of his preaching, he was imprisoned dozens of times, sometimes for a year or two at a time. He often used his confinement to write pamphlets and letters; some to leaders of other nations; some to his followers—whom he called "The Children of Light"—stating their position with clarity and boldness. From prison, he organized the people into groups called "meetings" and created a church administrative hierarchy that remains today. (See Chapter 4, "Quaker Meeting Organization," for an in-depth explanation of Meetings as organizational units.) He also wrote about his beliefs relating to peace in a document called the "Peace Testimony," which has remained the basis for the Quaker stand against war for more than 300 years. Fox strongly believed that his followers could not fulfill the mission of Christians, that of "answering that of God which exists in every man," and still support war efforts. He expected them to pattern their lives after the life of Jesus Christ.

Be patterns, be examples in all countries, places, islands, nations wherever you come; that your carriage and life may preach among all sorts of people, and to them; then you will come to walk cheerfully over the world, answering that of God in everyone; whereby in them you may be a blessing, and make the witness of God in them to bless you.

— George Fox

Continued Persecution Necessitates Record Keeping

In 1675, from his prison cell, George Fox created a new title for his followers. The group's new name became the "Religious Society of Friends." The London Yearly Meeting was created as an umbrella organization and to establish a visible and recognizable authority in support of the Friends. As more Friends felt compelled to share their beliefs with strangers, it became important to identify who, exactly, spoke with authority for the sect. The Quakers did not want to be accused unfairly because of individuals who might preach in the name of the Quakers but who held no authority to do so. Thus, in the 1680s, the Quakers began to keep records of members, including their names, ages, and other pertinent information. Sometimes in those records, you will see someone's name and the word "Minister" next to it. This was meant to illustrate that the Society had agreed that that person had authority to speak for the group as a whole. It did not mean he or she had any special dispensation as a member. It was more of an outward indication that the person belonged to the Society, had a special gift for speaking to crowds of people, and had the authority to do so. Thus, if a man or woman was arrested for speaking in public, the Society took responsibility for that individual's comments or actions only if he or she had the designation of "Minister."

Fox commissioned two Friends to collect the testimonies of persecuted Quakers as evidence of the unfair practices of both Church and State throughout England. This action led to the establishment of a committee called the "Meeting for Sufferings." The Meeting for Sufferings took on the role of administering funds for financial relief to the families of imprisoned Friends. [See *Selected Bibliography* in the Appendix for a book by Joseph Besse about the Quaker sufferings.]

The importance of accurate membership records also became apparent when families in

Certificates of Removal can aid in tracking the movements of Quaker ancestors. People rarely just left and moved to a new location without knowing the name of the meeting they planned to attend upon arrival. Sometimes, you can chart the journey of a Quaker family because the family's request for a certificate is written in the minutes in the former meeting, including the name of the new meeting. When they arrive, their names appear in minutes of the new meeting. (See Chapter 6, "Major Record Types," for details and examples.)

need, especially those who were new in town, came to the Society for financial assistance. The Friends wanted a mechanism that would allow them to help people yet not be taken advantage of by unscrupulous individuals. For that purpose, they provided letters of transit for Quakers who desired to move to a new location, whether this was across the ocean or to another town in their same country.

George Fox was married at the age of 45 to widow Margaret Fell, who had several grown children. His life was one of almost constant persecution for his writings and preaching. He died in 1691. His wife printed his journal, a wonderful view of his life and 45-year ministry, after his death. His good friend William Penn wrote the introduction. The *Journal of George Fox* continues to be printed today. It is estimated that 650,000 people, 10 percent of England's population at the time, were Quakers when Fox died. Nearly 13,000 had been imprisoned in the massive persecution imposed upon them. Another 200 were forced into slavery.

FIGURE 2-2: William Penn was an English Quaker who sought to construct a new society in the Pennsylvania Colony.

"The Holy Experiment"

William Penn was the son of Sir William Penn, who was an Admiral in the British Navy and friend to the king. William the younger was educated at the University of Oxford, and it was there that he started investigating various religious movements. During a period of time when the Quakers were considered heretics for going against the prevailing religions of the day, Penn became their champion. His law degree was helpful in pleading their cases to the magistrates of the day, and he used his considerable wealth to get dozens of Quakers released from prisons. Penn was just 37 years old when the king gave him land in the new Colonies as payment for his father's service in the British Navy. The land size amounted to roughly the size of England. Penn felt that it was a divine gift and proposed that it become a haven for his friends, the followers of the teachings of George Fox. He was finally in a position to provide a place for the Quakers to settle in the colonies and escape the brutality they were forced to suffer in England. In a letter to Friends, Penn humbly wrote:

My Friends:

"I wish you all happiness, here, and hereafter. These [notes] are to let you know that it hath pleased God, in his providence, to cast you within my lot and care. It is a business that, although I never undertook before, yet God hath given me an understanding of my duty, and an honest mind to do it uprightly. I hope you will not be troubled…for you are now fixed at the mercy of no governor that comes to make his fortune great; you shall be governed by laws of your own making and live a free, and if you will, a sober and industrious life. I shall not usurp the right of any, or oppress his person. God has furnished me with a better resolution and has given me his grace to keep it…"

Penn opened the Pennsylvania Colony in 1681 and founded the city of Philadelphia the following year to serve as the capital. Quakers emigrated by the thousands partly because Penn reduced the fees for the land, charging only 1 pence per acre for renters and £100 per 5000 acres for buyers. Within three months, he had sold 800,000 acres to well-to-do Quakers who were anxious for a new start in a safe place. An estimated 23,000 people left England and

Philadelphia is still called the "City of Brotherly Love."

Wales between 1681 and 1711 for the New World, with more coming from other locations. Penn called Pennsylvania the "Holy Experiment." The divinely inspired concept was to see if all people could live together in harmony, guided by the Holy Spirit, regardless of race, culture, wealth, or education.

Penn, who spoke German fluently, traveled to Germany and personally funded the cost of boats to pick up refugees from the Palatine region and give them free passage to the colony. The refugees were allowed to work off their passage over the course of several years, thereby making them the first indentured servants. The Germans were permitted to maintain their own language, religion, and culture as long as they lived in peace with the Quakers. They were what would come to be called the "Pennsylvania Dutch," a misnomer as they were from Deutschland, or Germany.

Penn hoped that Pennsylvania would be a profitable venture for himself and his family. Still, he vowed that he would never dishonor the divine gift of this land by exploiting either the natives or the immigrants, saying "I would not abuse His love, nor act unworthy of His providence, and so defile what came to me clean."

Penn's state charter, entitled "Frame of Government of Pennsylvania," was ground-breaking in nature and served to provide several inspired new concepts in governing. Besides limiting Penn's own power as governor, the charter included such new ideas as: freedom of worship, trial by jury, free elections, and more (see figure below). His document was based on the Magna Carta and was eventually used as the basis for portions of the U.S. Constitution, written nearly 100 years later. It affirmed ideas of equality and justice for all who consented to live within the laws.

Penn knew that religious persecution interfered with the smooth operation of commerce and property. He welcomed Jews, Anglicans, Mennonites, and Lutherans to the Pennsylvania

---

A Frame of Government for the Pennsylvania Colony

In 1681, William Penn wrote, "It is a clear and just thing, and my God who has given it me through many difficulties, will I believe, bless us and make this the seed of a nation."

Penn drew up document which he called, "A Frame of Government for the Pennsylvania Colony", which contained radical new ideas. Among them were the following:

❑ A "Charter of Liberties" which guaranteed a trial by jury, freedom of religion, freedom from unjust imprisonment and free elections.

❑ Penn limited his own power, thus laying a legal framework for a society where power was derived from the people;

❑ The new government would: have two houses, safeguard the rights of private property, promote free enterprise, and impose taxes fairly.

❑ The death penalty would be imposed only in two instances; treason and murder, rather than the two hundred+ instances under English law, and all cases would be tried before a jury of peers.

❑ Prisons would be progressive, attempting to correct through "workshops" rather than through hellish confinement.

❑ Swearing, lying, and drunkenness were forbidden as well as "idle amusements" such as gambling, revelry, masques, cock-fighting, and bear-baiting.

Penn borrowed concepts from John Locke as did Thomas Jefferson, but Penn added his own revolutionary idea—the use of amendments—to enable a written framework to evolve with the changing times. He hoped that an 'amendable' constitution would accommodate dissent and new ideas, and allow meaningful societal change without resorting to violent uprisings or revolution.

FIGURE 2-3: *The Frame of Government of Pennsylvania was a constitution drafted by William Penn for the Colony of Pennsylvania. The Frame of Government is viewed as an historical step in the design of democracy in America.*

Colony, and for many years, peace reigned among all sects. Even Catholics were allowed to pursue their religion and community life (unusual in the Colonies) as long as they agreed to abide by the civil laws of Philadelphia and surrounding communities.

References and Suggested Reading

1. Fox, George. *Journal of George Fox*, John Nickalls, editor, New York: Cambridge University Press, 1952, 2014

2. *Journal of George Fox,* London: Thomas Northcott, 1694, p. 12

3. Lippincott, Horace Mather. *Early Philadelphia: Its People, Life and Progress*. Philadelphia: J. B. Lippincott Company, 1917

4. Penn, William. *Passages from the Life and Writings of William Penn*, Friends Book Store, 1882

Quaker Migration, Significant Events, and Anti-Slavery Efforts

CHAPTER 3

Right is right, even if everyone is against it, and wrong is wrong, even if everyone is for it.
–William Penn

THIS CHAPTER OUTLINES THE MIGRATION of the Quakers, both those leaving the British Isles and those in the Colonies. If there are words or phrases unfamiliar to you, see Chapter 5, "Glossary of Early Quaker Terms and Concepts."

The Friends were a migratory people—some out of choice, others by necessity. It is helpful to try to imagine the circumstances and challenges that the Quakers faced during the time that your ancestor lived. Imagine the whole congregation discussing a move to a colony 1000 miles away or across an ocean. Perhaps you are elderly and can't make the trip, yet your long-time friends are leaving. Perhaps you are a Quaker woman who married a non-Quaker man who did not want to move. Perhaps you have several children and must make the move alone. Perhaps you and your wife have been arrested multiple times. Or, perhaps the constable closed your business for a trumped-up reason, and you are anxious to go the New World and start over. Perhaps you moved your family to a farm in South Carolina and freed your slaves, and now you are persecuted by your neighbors who boycott your farm and refuse to allow you to sell your goods. Do you uproot your family again and move with the Friends to a new state? This chapter will help you to picture yourself in these situations. Would you have the courage to do what they did?

There were several major migration periods for the Quakers. Here is an overview of those periods:

- **1660–1700:** Quakers migrate to America and establish yearly meetings in Rhode Island (New England Yearly Meeting), Philadelphia, Baltimore, Virginia, and New York. They have a strong presence in these states, economically and politically.

- **1700–1775:** Quakers move to the south (the Carolinas, Georgia, and Tennessee) and west toward eastern Ohio. This migration grows momentum as talk of revolution against England becomes more prevalent.

- **1776:** Quaker Loyalists migrate to Canada in opposition to the war.

- **1810–1825:** Quakers leave the Southern states in large numbers to escape a slave-based economy and settle in Ohio, Indiana, Illinois, and Michigan. These states, the former Northwest Territory, have been declared by Congress as non-slave states.

- **1827:** The Quaker movement endures several difficult schisms as Friends in America find themselves in disagreement over which leaders to follow and which doctrines are most important to the basic tenets of the Quaker religion.

- **1854:** Quakers from Indiana Yearly Meeting begin migrating west to Kansas and Nebraska. (The Kansas-Nebraska Act of 1854 creates the territories of Kansas and Nebraska, opening new lands for settlement.)

There are a couple of important points to remember about early Quaker migration:

1. Migration patterns generally emerge when the original minutes are consulted. However, for each theory created after reading of several families making similar moves, there are other

families who went in another direction. There was no one way of doing things, no rules, so don't expect any family to fit a pattern of migration.

2. These were people who were trying to figure out how to raise their families in peace and to live according to their Christian values. When settlers pushed the frontier farther and farther west in pursuit of freedom and land, Quakers were among the various groups of people moving in that direction. In fact, the federal government often called upon Quakers to help form good relations with the American Indian tribes.

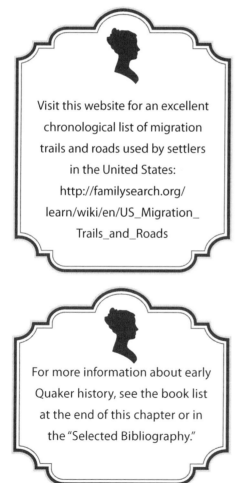

Visit this website for an excellent chronological list of migration trails and roads used by settlers in the United States: http://familysearch.org/learn/wiki/en/US_Migration_Trails_and_Roads

For more information about early Quaker history, see the book list at the end of this chapter or in the "Selected Bibliography."

The following timeline of Quaker events is designed to add context and color to their story, along with dates and locations. It is an easy way to see the steady growth of the Quaker movement as more Friends made the journey to America and as subsequent generations continued in the faith and traditions of their forefathers. It is an overview and not intended to be comprehensive; that is, it includes the events that were *most* impactful to the Quakers. There are many more events written by and about the early Quakers with details too extensive to include here.

Quaker Events Worth Noting

1656: Friends from England arrive in Boston to share their testimony. The Puritans do not welcome them. The Quakers are fined, harassed, mutilated, and several are even executed. The Quakers seek refuge in nearby Rhode Island. Governor Roger Williams, himself a former Puritan, permits them to stay. Several prominent Rhode Island families join the Quakers.

1657: Quakers are not welcome in the Virginia Colony. In fact, laws are passed to penalize ship captains who bring Quakers to Virginia and people who associate with Quakers. A small group of Friends build a meeting house in Nassawadox, VA.

1660s: Persecution continues against the Quakers in Massachusetts and some Friends are physically branded with an "H" for heretic. The death penalty is instituted for any Friends who return to the Massachusetts Colony after being banished. Some travel to the area that now comprises West Virginia, Virginia, and the Carolinas.

1661: The first General Meeting of Friends in America is held in Newport, RI. It eventually becomes the New England Yearly Meeting.

1666: Welsh and Irish Quakers begin to settle in South Carolina and Georgia.

1670: Two Friends in England, John Fenwick and Edward Billings, purchase East Jersey. Their intention is to provide a refuge for Quakers. Robert Barclay, a Scottish minister, is appointed as the first governor of the colony. Scottish Quakers immigrate to East Jersey in large numbers over the next decade.

1671: George Fox arrives in the Colonies, along with a dozen other Quakers from England. They go to the Carolinas to help establish new meetings there. Fox spends time traveling along the coast, preaching and strengthening the scattered Quakers and others. Before his return to England, he goes to Rhode Island to formally create the New England Yearly Meeting, which starts with seven small congregations.

1672: The Baltimore Yearly Meeting is established. By 1700, there are about 3000 Quakers in Maryland.

1673: The Virginia Yearly Meeting is established.

1681: William Penn accepts a land grant from King Charles of England. It comprises the Pennsylvania and Delaware territories. He opens the colony to the Quakers to help them escape the persecution they experienced in other colonies.

1682: William Penn and other Quakers begin arriving in the Pennsylvania Colony. Soon there are thousands living around Philadelphia and along the Delaware River. Most of them are from England (London and Bristol, as well as western, midland, and northern counties), Wales, Ireland, Germany (lower Rhineland), France, Denmark, Finland, and the Netherlands. They are mostly wealthy English Quakers who sold their property in England and sought refuge in the New World to escape severe persecution. Penn personally invites artisans, craftsmen, and architects to bring their skills and ideas to the colony. He promises them work for good wages and 50 acres of land to set up their own homes and orchards. As a result, within 15 years, the city of Philadelphia boasts over 2000 stately, brick, 3-story homes.

1686: The Philadelphia Yearly Meeting is established, comprising most monthly meetings in New Jersey and Pennsylvania.

1696: The New York Yearly Meeting is established.

1698: The North Carolina Yearly Meeting is established.

1700: The first meeting in Canada is established.

1725: Friends from New Jersey, Maryland, Pennsylvania, and New England begin to migrate south via the Great Wagon Road, settling in along the Roanoke Gap in Virginia and on to the Carolinas.

1763: With the end of the French and Indian War, Quakers begin migrating from eastern to western portions of Pennsylvania and beyond the Allegheny Mountains. Penn and the early Quakers establish such a good rapport with the American Indians who live within the confines of the colony that, generations later, these Quakers are welcomed as they move west. The Mississippi River Valley is now back in the hands of the English and open for settlement.

Late 1760s: Quakers from Pennsylvania swarm to the central portions of the Carolinas to establish themselves among the vast Southern plantations. They soon realize that slavery is a difficult issue to ignore. They find it impossible to compete economically with slave labor. But the Quakers find it even more difficult to deal with slavery on a spiritual level.

Early 1770s: Quakers from New England, eastern New York, and central Pennsylvania, who are not able to support the Revolutionary War, move either north to Canada or south to settle in the western part of the Carolinas and eastern Tennessee.

1777: The Baltimore Yearly Meeting establishes a new practice of disowning any member holding slaves. In **1784**, the Virginia Yearly Meeting makes the same ruling. By **1790**, all Quaker slaveholders have released their slaves.

1780: Friends from South Carolina begin to migrate to settlements in eastern Tennessee.

1785: Congress enacts the Northwest Ordinance in **1787**, which guarantees that neither slavery nor involuntary servitude is to be permitted in any of the territory north of the Ohio River. This act appeals to the Quakers in the South who have freed their slaves and are struggling with an economy dependent on slavery. When the Northwest Territory opens in **1795**, Quakers are among those who move to the "New West" not only from the South, but also from New Jersey, eastern Pennsylvania, northern Virginia, and New York.

1790: Friends in New England continue to migrate into western and upper-state New York and along the border with Canada. Within 20 years, there are 9 meetings established in the area. The result, in some cases, is the movement of entire congregations from eastern New York and New England.

1810: An entire meeting from North Carolina moves to the Short Creek area of Ohio above Wheeling, WV, and establishes a new meeting there. An estimated 800 Quaker families move to the Ohio area by **1820**. There are no members of the Society of Friends remaining in Georgia and South Carolina after about the year **1830**. The state of Virginia is depleted of Quakers by that time, as well. Although they were accompanied by many who were not Quakers. By **1850**, one-third of the population of Indiana were said to be made up of native North Carolinians and their children.

1813: The Ohio Yearly Meeting is established, comprising all quarterly meetings west of the Allegheny Mountains and in the Indiana Territory. It is estimated that there are nearly 20,000 Quakers in the Ohio Yearly Meeting, a full one-quarter of which have come from the Philadelphia Yearly Meeting.

1821: The Indiana Yearly Meeting is established by Friends who migrate from Ohio into Indiana and Illinois.

1827: After 150 years of living their lives in a fairly united manner and according to the basic tenets of the Quaker religion in America, growing ideological differences break the Society of Friends into two factions—the "Hicksite" (following Elias Hicks) and the Orthodox. The split, known as the "Great Separation of 1827," takes place in the Philadelphia Yearly Meeting. Soon after, the New York, Baltimore, and Ohio Yearly Meetings also split. See more about these factions in Chapter 4, "Quaker Meeting Organization."

1834: The first Quaker settlers arrive in Salem, IA. They are from the Indiana Yearly Meeting. The trip from Indiana takes 4–6 weeks by wagon.

1835: As more people move westward, Quakers establish the Western Yearly Meeting to serve Friends in western Indiana and eastern Illinois.

1861: With the coming of the Civil War, Quakers are not in the same position as most of the other citizens of the United States who were choosing sides. They gave up their slaves (or left the faith) and moved to non-slave states many years prior to the first shot being fired at Fort Sumter.

1863: The Iowa Yearly Meeting is established, comprising 45 meetings and 5 quarterly meetings. Within 30 years, there are over 12,000 Quakers settled here.

Quakers and Slavery

Slavery used to be an accepted custom in the world, and many Quakers owned slaves. However, when they started the new colony, Quaker founders felt inspired to strongly encourage Friends to stop owning slaves and become leaders in stopping the institution of slavery in the Colonies. The slow but steady march toward the freeing of slaves in America began with the Quakers in the year 1688.

Quakers were educated, middle-class merchants, who were often quite prosperous in their business ventures and felt duty-bound to follow the local laws - except in the case of slavery. Many of the early Quakers were determined to live according to the dictates of their Christian values, which meant that every man was a child of God and had the right to be free.

The Pennsylvania Anti-Slavery Society and the Manumission Society of North Carolina are two examples of how the Quakers organized to try and persuade their own members, as well as non-Quakers, to free their slaves. There are many discussions documented in the meeting minutes indicating the search that Friends conducted to find a way to obey the state laws regarding the slave trade (which were getting harsher with each passing year) and yet continue their efforts to free

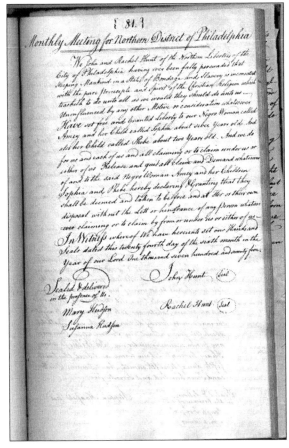

FIGURE 3-1: Image from Philadelphia Manusmission Book. With permission from Haverford College Library, Haverford PA, Quaker Collection, 1250, S2.15

slaves. Quakers in the South gathered funds to buy slaves—as families, if possible—and manumit them, bringing them under the care of the meeting. The legislatures of the Southern states created quite a backlash against these Quaker manumissions and gave county sheriffs the authority to pick up freed slaves and sell them again on the courthouse steps.

In response to these legislative acts, Friends helped to create the Underground Railroad, sending the slaves north to freedom through a secret network of sympathetic farmers. The Manumission Society of North Carolina also sent former slaves to freedom on the island of Haiti.

Be on the lookout for manumission records. Meetings in most states were heavily involved in the emancipation of slaves. Several manumission books have been scanned and can be found online; check the catalog on the Swarthmore or Haverford College websites.

Though their lives were in constant danger and they were met with a storm of opposition, Southern Quakers were determined to boldly proceed against slavery. Those actions caused obvious friction and resentment for Quakers living in slave states, and by 1820, they had largely migrated out of the South.

Following is a short timeline showing the Quaker involvement in the freeing of all slaves in America.

1688: Quakers in Germantown (now a suburb of Philadelphia) make the first recorded protest against slavery. Quakers, as a whole, become more publicly vocal against the institution of slavery.

1696: The Philadelphia Yearly Meeting officially discourages Friends from participating in slavery. This was the first recorded occurrence in which the Philadelphia Yearly Meeting addressed the slave trade and took an anti-slavery stance on the issue.

1715: The New England Yearly Meeting declares that the possession of slaves or participation in any form of slavery is grounds for disownment from the religion.

1774: Thomas Newby from Perquimans Monthly Meeting in North Carolina becomes the first Southern Quaker to publicly request the advice and assistance of Friends in the weighty and important affair of giving slaves their liberty.

1777: The North Carolina Yearly Meeting (covering the Carolinas, Georgia, and eastern Tennessee) admonishes all Friends to manumit their slaves. Newby and 10 other Quakers free their 134 slaves. As a result, major repercussions ensue from the state legislature.

Late 1700s: Quakers help establish the Underground Railroad, enabling slaves to reach the

Northern states and freedom. In **1786**, George Washington writes that one of his runaway slaves is helped by a "society of Quakers, formed for such purposes."

1787: In Britain, Quakers establish the first recognized anti-slavery movement and directly assist William Wilberforce in his crusade in Parliament to end the transport of slaves by British ships. (The movie *Amazing Grace* [2006] recounts these events.)

Early 1800s: Whole congregations of Quakers leave the South and move to Indiana and Ohio when Congress declares them to be non-slave states. By **1850**, there are almost no Quaker families remaining in the Southern states and an estimated 30% of the population of Indiana is made up of former North Carolinians.

Movement of Quaker Families from VA and NC Yearly Meetings to Ohio & Indiana in the early 1800s
Showing the Number of Families Granted Certificates of Removal, where they moved to and when they left.

Monthly Meetings	Before 1801	1801 to 1810		1811 to 1820		1821 to 1830		1831 to 1840		1841 to 1850		1851 to 1860	
	Moved to PA	Moved to Ohio	Moved to Indiana	Moved to Ohio	Moved to Indiana	Moved to Ohio	Moved to Indiana	Moved to Ohio	Moved to Indiana	Moved to Ohio	Moved to Indiana	Moved to Ohio	Moved to Indiana
From Virginia YM													
Alexandria (1802-1851)				4		2		8		14			
Cedar Creek (1738-1842)				9		5		2					
Crooked Run (1787-1807)	18	53	16 (to PA)										
Fairfax (1744-1926)	9	22		2	2 (to PA)	4		1	2 (to PA)	2			
Goose Creek, North (1794-1814)	20	31		16	1	12	9	38	2	3	1	4	1
Gravelly Run (1801-1832)						39	2	5					
Hopewell (1785-1850)	62	20	18 (to PA)	36	1	14		10	2	3	3	1	
South River (1801-40)		44	15 (to PA)	42	2	19	3	4					
Western Branch (1806-36)		8		13	2	7	3	8	12				
White Oak Swamp (1811-36)				11		15		11	1				
From North Carolina YM													
Bush River, SC (1801-1807)		111											
Cane Creek, NC (1796-1837)		48			31		47		38				
Great Contentnea (1800-1843)	2	31		5	8	1	48	1	20				
Core Sound (1793-1840)	13	12		3	27	1	20	2	24		3		9
Deep River (1808-1850)					1	1	6	10	18	2	30		3
Dover (1802-1850)							12		12		13		
Hopewell (1821-1848)													
Jack Swamp (1805-1812)		17		9									
Mt. Pleasant, VA (1802-1825)		43	1	51	10	2	2						
New Garden (1754-)		12	1	31	36	1	61	1	19	7		1	25
Piney Grove, SC (1805-1815)		2		15	16								
Piney Woods (1802-1830)		6		4	6	1	8		4				
Rich Square (1802-1960)	1	11		2	2	1	7		2	1	1		2
Spring (1830-1838)									22				
Springfield (1785-1850)		24		6	44	1	39	1	26		3		
Sutton's Creek (1812-1835)					88		5		11				
Symon's Creek (1803-1854)		8		1	22	1	7		7		7		1
Westfield (1801-1838)		37		10	7				5				
Wrightsborough, GA (1773-1805)		19											

FIGURE 3-2: Movement of Quaker Families from VA and NC Yearly Meetings to Ohio & Indiana in the early 1800s. Some data extracted from Southern Quakers and Slavery: A Study in Institutional History, Stephen B. Weeks, Baltimore: Johns Hopkins Press, 1896.

References and Suggested Reading

1. Elliott, Errol T. *Quakers on the American Frontier.* Elgin, IL: The Brethren Press, 1969

2. Elliott, Wendy. *A Historical Overview of American Quaker Migration,* 1987

3. Heiss, Willard C. *Quaker Migration in the United States.* World Conference on Records and Genealogical Seminar, 1969

4. Hull, William Isaac. *William Penn and the Dutch Quaker Migration to Pennsylvania.* Swarthmore College, 1935

5. Levy, Barry. *Quakers and the American Family: British Settlement in the Delaware Valley.* New York: Oxford University Press, 1988

6. Lippincott, Horace Mather. *Early Philadelphia: Its People, Life and Progress,* Philadelphia: J.P. Lippincott Company, 1917

7. McVetty, Suzanne, CG. *Records of the Society of Friends (Quakers), New York Yearly Meeting,* originally published in The NYG&B Newsletter, Fall 1997

8. Myers, Albert Cook. *Immigration of the Irish Quaker into Pennsylvania,*

9. Quaker-roots archives on www.rootsweb.ancestry.com

10. Weeks, Stephen B. Ph.D. *Southern Quakers and Slavery,* Baltimore/Johns Hopkins Press, 1896

11. Worrall, Arthur J. *Quakers in the Colonial Northeast,* Hanover, New Hampshire, 1980

Quaker Meeting Organization

CHAPTER 4

*Patience and Diligence,
like Faith, remove mountains.*
–William Penn

THIS CHAPTER EXPLAINS THE ORGANIZATION of the Quaker religion. An examination of the function of each of the four administrative levels, together with a short discussion regarding a major split that occurred in 1827, will assist in determining exactly where to find the most informative records for researching individual Quakers.

Membership

In the early years, there was no formal membership process. They were friends meeting together—that's all. Others knew by your *behavior* whether or not you were a believer and genuinely seeking the truth in your life. During the first several decades, this Christian behavior sometimes included your willingness to accept the penalties of nonconformity—imprisonment, beatings, impoverishment, slavery and possibly death. Eventually, the need for formal membership rolls came about, and starting in about 1650, Friends started keeping track of who their members were. Members were received into membership in one of several ways: 1) by presenting a certificate from another monthly meeting; 2) by their own request for membership; 3) by birthright (both parents are members); 4) by Letter of Transfer from another denomination; 5) by being transferred into a newly organized monthly meeting from an older one, in which case the member is called a Charter Member of the new meeting.

By virtue of membership in a monthly meeting, Friends also become members of a regional gathering and the yearly meeting. All members have the privilege and the responsibility to participate in decision-making within each body. Within its own area of responsibility, each body is autonomous. Friends do not attend regional meetings and yearly meeting as instructed delegates of their monthly meetings but join others in worship and decisions that respond to the moving of the Spirit in that time and place.

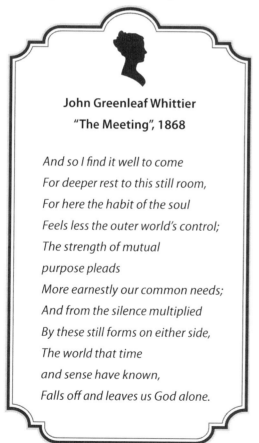

John Greenleaf Whittier
"The Meeting", 1868

And so I find it well to come
For deeper rest to this still room,
For here the habit of the soul
Feels less the outer world's control;
The strength of mutual
purpose pleads
More earnestly our common needs;
And from the silence multiplied
By these still forms on either side,
The world that time
and sense have known,
Falls off and leaves us God alone.

Weekly Worship Service

The Meeting for Worship was the core and center of the religion. It was the worshipping congregation with a physical address, much the same as a parish. It was at this level that the church family met to interact with each other on a weekly basis. Every member of The Society of Friends was registered as a member of a Meeting for Worship and of the monthly meeting to which it belonged. The Quakers called it "going to meeting," just like members of other faiths say "going to church" or "going to synagogue." The service was held on Sunday morning and in the early years, a mid-week meeting was also held. Quakers worshipped in silence, meditating on the words of Christ and on their particular circumstances, petitioning the Lord in silent prayer. They based the worship service on the Biblical scripture from Matthew 18:20, "For where two or three have gathered together in my name, there am I in the midst of them." Meetings for worship were at first held informally at someone's home or in the countryside. There was no passing of a plate for money; there was no passing of a physical sacrament, or music, or sermons. The congregation "centered down," meaning that each person focused on his or her own meditation, "waiting upon the Lord" for personal revelation.

If worshippers felt "moved upon," they stood up to share their thoughts. This sharing was a solemn responsibility because they were "breaking the silence" of the others. For this reason, their comments were usually brief. Another person might stand up after time passed, to either add to the previous comments or share a new thought. There were usually no more than three or four people who broke the silence during the hour, thus allowing others in attendance to settle back into silence and concentrate on their own thoughts. Sometimes, when a person sharing a message was becoming long-winded and the meeting needed to return to silence, an Elder might stand and quietly say, "Thank thee Friend, I believe that we have received the weight of thy message".

When the religion began to grow and formal meeting houses were designed, the congregation sat on wooden benches. Benches in the meetinghouse were usually set up facing each other so that there was no focal point, like an altar or a pulpit, as is usually the case in other denominations, Elders, both men and women, generally sat on the "facing bench", the first row of seats on one side. The elders were usually more mature (weighty) Friends who kept a watchful eye over the spiritual life of the meeting. It was their responsibility to see that the messages given were doctrinally sound and in keeping with the discipline of the Society. The Elders are the ones who discerned that it was time to end the meeting and indicated it by shaking hands. When meeting ended, most attendees shared refreshments in the Fellowship Hall, attended the weekly business meeting, or both. If members wanted to contribute funds to the church, they did so quietly to the Clerk of the meeting, which was a rotating administrative responsibility not attached to a particular skill or position in the congregation.

Quakers tended to adopt more traditional practices for their worship services as time passed and as they moved west. Occasionally, when there were only a few Quaker families living in a settlement, they would hire a traveling preacher. They passed a plate in order to pay him, and music became part of the service. These worship services became known as "programmed" meetings and were more prevalent in the West, usually in areas far from the central body of Quakers.

Quakers called their buildings meeting houses, rather than "churches." Founder George Fox was opposed to using the word "church" to describe the physical building of worship because he used the term "church" as it is used in the Bible, to describe the body of worshippers. Hundreds of Quaker meeting houses were built in England and then in the Colonies, beginning in the mid-1600s. Each meeting house was usually owned by the Meeting for Worship. (See Chapter 12, "Meeting Houses and Quaker Burial Grounds," for a more detailed description of Quaker meeting houses, including website links to view photographs online.)

Administrative Structure

George Fox and his wife Margaret Fell created the religion's organizational structure in about 1660, with no central governing body, which makes the growth of the religion even more impressive. There were four organizational levels, with each group conducting the business assigned to that level. The largest body was the yearly meeting. It was composed of quarterly meetings, which were composed of monthly meetings. The lowest organizational level was usually known as the "preparative" meeting.

TIP: When researching a meeting, look for the terms "set off" and "laid down" to determine when it started and under which monthly meeting it originally formed. Establishing these date ranges can help you verify whether your ancestors were members of a particular meeting.

Preparative Meetings

A Preparative meeting was the business side of the Meeting for Worship, a close-knit spiritual community of Friends, much the same as a congregation in any religion. Preparative meetings each covered a specific geographic area and were grouped under the care of a monthly meeting, which was usually nearby geographically. The business meetings at this level were mostly concerned with the building and grounds and took no disciplinary actions. It could, however, settle minor offenses and "prepare" any issues regarding violations of Quaker Discipline to the monthly meeting to which it reported. Members were encouraged to be present and to help with the business of the meeting. The preparative meeting appointed delegates to the monthly meeting, who reported back to the meeting. As congregations grew in size and earned positive reports from the oversight committee, the preparative meetings were permitted to become their own monthly meetings in a process called being "set off." If membership numbers began to decline, a preparative meeting was discontinued in a process called being "laid down."

Monthly Meetings

Friends have kept the power of decision in religious matters as close as possible to the primary worship group and the individual. The monthly meeting has both the freedom of action and the responsibility in matters of membership not given to other levels. Monthly meetings were composed of the preparative meetings in a small geographical area. Monthly meetings had no physical address or meeting house associated with them because they were administrative in nature. Monthly meetings rotated to different meeting houses to make it fair for all the attending delegates.

The name of the monthly meeting may have the same name as a Meeting for Worship, or it may have a different name. The monthly meeting is a separate entity from any Meeting for Worship under its care.

Minutes were taken at the business meetings on the monthly meeting level, and it is these minutes that hold the most genealogical information. The records of members of all types of meetings were kept by the monthly (business) meeting. The monthly meeting were attended by delegates sent by their sub-ordinate meetings–the Meetings for Worship and their Preparative (business) Meeting. The monthly meeting was the executive body of the Quaker administrative organization. It was a business meeting which administered the affairs of its sub-ordinate meetings; there were usually several under the control of each monthly meeting.

This level had responsibility for member records, including births, deaths, burials, marriages, disownments, and members received and released, for all Preparative Meetings belonging to it. It was responsible for the supervision of schools and burying grounds, dispensing of charitable funds, and creating reports for the quarterly meeting. Many monthly meetings had trustees who held titles to property donated to the Friends, and who supervised funds and investments. (see Chapter 5, "Glossary of Early Quaker Terms and Concepts"),

From the earliest days, men and women held separate business meetings at the monthly meeting level. George Fox felt impressed that women should meet separately from the men to enable them to discuss issues openly. He felt that women would be the most informed about issues in the home and family and empowered them to make decisions regarding them. The two groups discussed essentially the same issues, and sometimes business conducted by the women was referred to the men's meeting for their consideration. Often small committees in both the men's and women's meetings were assigned to investigate issues and report their findings at the next meeting; these assignments and their respective findings were recorded in the minutes. These reports and discussions shed considerable light on the various aspects of Quaker membership and often provide fascinating reading.

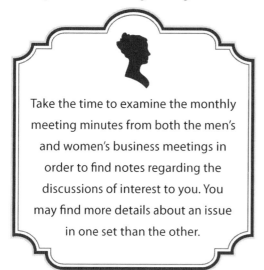

Take the time to examine the monthly meeting minutes from both the men's and women's business meetings in order to find notes regarding the discussions of interest to you. You may find more details about an issue in one set than the other.

Each monthly meeting had a Recording Clerk who kept careful minutes of the discussions and decisions made. It was his or her responsibility to ascertain the collective will of the meeting and record it. Friends worked very hard to reach a consensus, and would sometimes "agree to disagree" and shelve the matter until another time in order not to offend or make decisions that were not agreeable to all parties. Sometimes, many months passed before matters were decided on, if they could not reach a consensus.

You will find marriage certificates, requests for Certificates of Removal, disciplinary actions, etc., written into both sets of minutes, although sometimes there is more detail written by some clerks than others.

The Clerk of the meeting took his or her job very seriously. The records and history of the meeting were entrusted to their keeping, sometimes for many years. In fact, when the Separation of 1827 created a split in the congregations, some clerks would not share the record books they had labored over and instead kept them in their possession. You may find statements in the records where the former clerk from one side of the schism would not allow the new clerk from the opposing congregation to even *see* the record book, forcing the other group to try and create a new record book from memory. (A more detailed description of the Separation of 1827 appears at the end of this chapter.)

Quarterly Meetings

There are some matters on which some agreement among monthly meetings is essential to the proper functioning of the Society. The third level comprising the Quaker church administration was the quarterly meeting, created from constituents who represented all the monthly meetings in a geographic area. Quarterly meetings convened four times a year and either settled issues that could not be resolved on a local level or placed them on the agenda of the yearly meeting. This body also had the capacity to govern on issues that involved several monthly meetings, such as Friends nursing homes or schools.

Meeting names were often derived from the Bible, from nearby locations such as towns, or from nearby bodies of water or mountains. Popular names for meetings often appear in multiple states or regions, so take care in your research to determine that you are looking at the records for the meeting in the correct county and state. For example, there were 21 meetings with the name "Salem."

Yearly Meetings

The Yearly Meeting is the law-giving body governing all other levels. The annual meeting is attended by delegates from each quarterly meeting, and was a conference held over a period of several days and attended by thousands of people. The group discussed issues of weighty significance, like changes in policy and direction, and addressed issues that the quarterly meetings submitted for the agenda. The decisions reached by the yearly meetings were binding upon all quarterly and monthly meetings in their jurisdiction. In an effort to maintain harmony, if a decision could not be reached by a consensus of the group, the issue was held over until the next meeting, one year later.

Quaker meeting organization changed a bit in 1827; the rest of this chapter explains how the changes affect the process of doing Quaker research.

A great collection of information for monthly meetings in North America is available on Tom Hill's website at Quakermeetings.com. Hill has compiled information for over 2000 meetings, including Quaker meetings in Canada.

The Separation of 1827 and Its Effect on the Quaker Records

After the Revolutionary War, some Quakers, mostly those living in larger cities and, therefore, more affected by the new "evangelical" mood of the country, began to question the strict code of the Quaker Book of Discipline. They became disenchanted with the old governing principles and tried to bring reform and more modern practices into the religion. These Quakers were several generations removed from the founders of the religion; those who had sacrificed their lives to establish it. In an attempt to preserve the original faith, the Elders of the Philadelphia Yearly Meeting made a well-meaning but ultimately heavy-handed attempt to suppress this reform. After nearly two centuries of living their lives according to the basic tenets outlined by its founders, the Society of Friends in the United States came under the weight of several pressures. These pressures created a split in 1827 that broke the Society into two groups. This severe schism remained in place for 130 years.

If your Quaker ancestors lived during the early 1800s, they most likely had to choose between two factions within the Society of Friends. Sometimes, families were divided over it. Sometimes, whole meetings decided that they would make the choice together in order to preserve their close connections with each other. There were heated debates over the significance of that choice during monthly meetings, as indicated in their minutes.

Elias Hicks, a longtime Friend and "traveling minister," was a farmer and family man who lived in Long Island, NY. He felt strongly about what he saw happening in the Quaker religion and often spoke out in an effort to try to stop what he felt was a drift from the core beliefs outlined by George Fox and other early founders. Congregations debated the issues; the "Hicksites" believed in continuing revelation, and the "Orthodox" believed that true Quaker practice relied heavily on the written word of the Bible.

Within a short amount of time, nearly two-thirds of members of the Philadelphia Yearly Meeting sided with the Hicksite faction, and eventually the five largest yearly meetings were split in two; Baltimore, Indiana, New York, Ohio, and Philadelphia Yearly Meetings. It was a very difficult time for the Quakers; more splits took place on both sides as they struggled to find and re-establish the core of their beliefs. During the last half of the 19th century, many of the Orthodox meetings were discontinued due to declining membership.

The Effect on Records

The effect the Separation of 1827 had on the records presents Quaker researchers with an interesting dilemma. Instantly, there were two monthly meetings with the *same name*, one Hicksite, the other Orthodox. When the Hicksite and Orthodox branches split, each side disowned the members of the other side. However, there was only one set of record books, so one side (usually the Orthodox) had to recreate their member lists. Care must be taken to determine which records you are researching.

The two groups sometimes met in the same meeting house but would enter through differ-

Rancocas Friends Meeting

When the Separation of 1827 occurred, the Rancocas Meeting Hicksite Friends retained the old brick meeting house, built in 1772. This required the Rancocas Meeting Orthodox Friends to find other accommodations and for a time, they worshiped in the room over the blacksmith shop. Eventually, the Hicksites invited the Orthodox to occupy the eastern end of the brick meeting, and erected a frame wall to divide the meeting room into two spaces, each using a different entrance door. The Rancocas meeting house remains in active use today, although the dividing wall was removed in the 1950s when the Friends united once more.

FIGURE 4-1: Friends in Rancocas Meeting eventually found a solution-two entrances.

ent doorways at different times on Sunday. In some cases, the meeting name was retained but a location was added to the title to distinguish it from the other (for example, the Wilmington Monthly Meeting at West Street [Hicksite Meeting] or the Wilmington Monthly Meeting at Harrison Street [Orthodox Meeting].

For more information on this subject, two pamphlets written during the time are available online. One of the pamphlets is pro-Hicksite, and the other is pro-Orthodox, but an anonymous person published both, possibly because the author did not get the required clearance from his or her meeting before publishing. The pamphlets are available on the Quaker Heritage Press website: http://www.qhpress.org/texts/h-o/index.html.

After the split, the New York Yearly Meeting created the "Census of Members of the New York Yearly Meeting at the Time of the Separation of 1828." (The list is available in book form through your local library or on Amazon.com). It is a list of the 19,000 members in the New York Yearly Meeting at the time of Separation in 1828. It includes both Orthodox and Hicksite branches and indicates the side with which each member affiliated. The members were from meetings in New York; Vermont; Connecticut; Berkshire County, Massachusetts; and several meetings in Canada. New York Yearly Meeting was the only yearly meeting to undertake such a project.

Pay close attention to the lists of members in the meeting record books. If you find that the names and birthdates are all in the same handwriting and appear to be written all at the same time, then you are most likely looking at a reconstructed membership list, and it is most likely an Orthodox record book. This is important information, because you may see that an ancestor was disowned on a certain date. This information may cause you to stop researching that name in the records thinking that the trail has ended. But all that may be needed is to find the Hicksite membership records for the same meeting, where the information for that ancestor was still being recorded.

In Summary

Membership registers began to appear more regularly after the newly split congregations struggled to comply with the requirement to record who was actually attending their meetings. These registers are a compilation of all known information about each individual. You will likely find your Quaker ancestor in either the Hicksite or Orthodox registers, depending on where he and his family stood in the conflict at the time.

The Hicksite-Orthodox separation was the largest of the splits but was followed by a number of smaller and more regional splits in the 19th and early 20th centuries. By the end of the 19th century, most Friends were either Hicksite or Orthodox, but there were also Wilburite, Conservative, Progressive, Primitive, Otisite, Kingite, and other splinter groups among American Quakers. As splinter groups formed and then disbanded, the records for members of these groups did not often survive.

References and Suggested Reading

1. "A Short History of Conservative Friends," www.snowcamp.org/shocf/shocf.html
2. Bacon, Margaret H. *The Quiet Rebels, the Story of the Quakers in America*, Basic Books, Inc. New York, 1969
3. Bliss, Forbush. *Elias Hicks: Quaker Liberal,* New York: Columbia University Press, 1956
4. Eckert, Jack. *Guide to the Records of the Philadelphia Yearly Meeting,* 1989
5. Hodgson, William. *The Society of Friends in the Nineteenth Century: A Historical View of the Successive Convulsions and Schisms Therein during that Period.* Philadelphia, 1875-1876. Vol I, p. 307
6. McVetty, Suzanne C.G. *Records of the Society of Friends (Quakers), New York Yearly Meeting,* originally published in The NYG&B Newsletter, Fall 1997

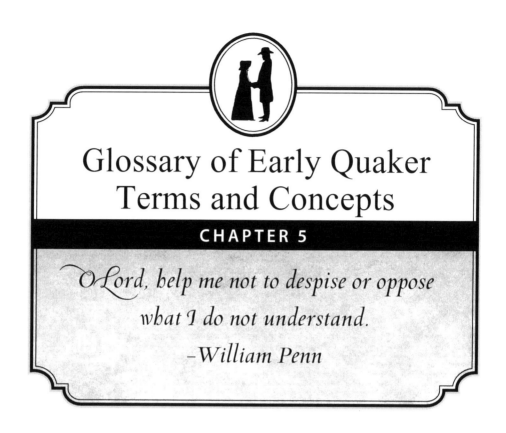

Glossary of Early Quaker Terms and Concepts

CHAPTER 5

O Lord, help me not to despise or oppose what I do not understand.

–William Penn

THE EARLY QUAKERS USED TERMS and phrases that are often confusing to researchers. This chapter explains the unique vernacular in an effort to assist in navigating the records.

Glossary

Acknowledgements and Apologies: A humble, formal, written statement of apology by a member of the meeting, for having acted contrary to the rules of discipline. For example: "Dear Friends, Having behaved inconsistent with our Christian profession by _____, which I sincerely condemn, I hope to continue under the care of the meeting." These are sometimes listed in a separate Book of Acknowledgements but are usually found in the monthly meeting minutes.

Baptism and Christening: There was no physical baptism or christening in the Quaker religion.

George Fox did not feel that there needed to be an actual sprinkling or immersion into water to become a true follower of Christ.

Birthright Friend: A person born to parents who were members of the early Quaker faith was considered a birthright member. This membership could be lost by misconduct, but otherwise it was a lifetime condition unless the person requested that his or her name be removed from the membership rolls.

Births and Deaths: Since the 1850s or so, vital records have generally been recorded in separate membership books. But early Quaker birth and death records were usually arranged by family surname and were often recorded after a family's arrival at the meeting. Deaths of adult members were often not recorded, especially in meetings without any burial grounds and where no membership books were kept. Though of immense value, the birth and death records are often not comprehensive. However, they are all that exist for that time period and are wonderful if you are able to find your ancestor in them.

Burial: Most of the time, meeting minutes discussed burials—not deaths—of members, although the passing of a prominent Friend was occasionally documented in the minutes. There was usually a separate book of burials kept at the preparatory meeting level, which is where the burial ground would have been. The names in the burial books were listed chronologically and often had the birthdates of the deceased as well as his or her spouse's name.

Dates and Calendar: Early Friends objected to the names of the days and months in the English language and considered them to be of heathen origin. Sunday was called as such by the Saxons because it was the day they sacrificed to the sun; Monday was the day on which they sacrificed to the moon; Thursday was the day on which they sacrificed to the god Thor, etc. Quakers thought it inconsistent for Christians to continue using the names of heathen idols. In an effort to distance themselves from these references, they created their own calendar terms using numbers, which seemed to them to be the most rational approach. Days of the week were known as "First Day" for Sunday, "Second Day" for Monday, and so forth. Quakers attended "First Day" school, not Sunday school. They used no other names but these, either in their spoken conversation or in their letters. The Quakers adopted the Gregorian calendar later than most people. The London

Yearly Meeting sent instructions to all Quakers stating that starting with December 1751, the calendar was to reflect the following changes:

The	Pre-1752	Month Called		shall be reckoned as the	1752	month of the next and every succeeding year.
	Eleventh		January		First	
	Twelfth		February		Second	
	First		March		Third	
	Second		April		Fourth	
	Third		May		Fifth	
	Fourth		June		Sixth	
	Fifth		July		Seventh	
	Sixth		August		Eighth	
	Seventh		September		Ninth	
	Eighth		October		Tenth	
	Ninth		November		Eleventh	
	Tenth		December		Twelfth	

FIGURE 5-1: The London Yearly Meeting sent instructions to all Quakers stating that starting with December 1751, the calendar was to reflect these changes..

This chart shows the pre-1752 and post-1752 names of the months, which are found in the Quaker records. For a deeper discussion about the calendar and how it impacts Quaker research, see Chapter 9, "Quaker Calendar and Dates."

Certificate of Removal: Traveling ministers, grooms going to their brides' meetings for the wedding ceremony, and families or individuals moving from one meeting to another were all expected to request a Certificate of Removal. The monthly meeting prepared this "traveling document" upon request if the person was a member in good standing with the meeting. The certificate vouched for the member or family, stating that they were leaving behind no outstanding debts or unresolved issues. This document was especially important for single Friends who wanted to marry under the care of the new meeting. Without a certificate, the meeting had a difficult time knowing if they could "clear" a person for marriage. You may see references in the minutes to those who arrived without certificates and the difficulties the new meeting had as a result.

The granting meeting recorded these certificates in the general minutes or sometimes in volumes kept specifically for certificates granted. They were also recorded in the minute books of the receiving meeting. They are sometimes found in "miscellaneous loose papers."

Clearness: Word describing a process through which the influence of the Spirit of God was discerned.

Clerks, Committees, and Other Positions of Responsibility: A nominating committee, chosen by meeting members, suggested suitable people to serve as Clerk, Recording Clerk, Treasurer, and several committees, including Overseers, Ministry and Worship, Funerals, and Religious Education. They served for a determined length of time when appointed by the monthly meeting.

- The **Clerk** presided at business meetings and carried out instructions of the meeting, including tracking the births, marriages, and deaths of members.

- The **Recording Clerk** took minutes of business meetings and submitted them at the next meeting.

- The **Treasurer** was responsible for the custody and disbursement of the meeting's funds. He or she reported regularly and had accounts audited annually. Trustees were also appointed to take care of these funds.

- The **Meeting Recorder** kept track of membership, giving reports to the meeting as well as to the quarterly and yearly meetings, when requested.

- The **Overseers Committee** served for a predetermined time and was responsible for the pastoral care of the meeting, similar to administrative duties that a minister does in Protestant religions. They received letters of application for membership and considered them carefully before they were presented to the monthly meeting. Sometimes an ad hoc committee of oversight was appointed to visit the prospective member and report back.

- The **Ministry and Worship Committee** had duties similar to the spiritual part of what a minister does in a Protestant religion.

Concern (synonym would be a "prompting"): An impression felt through the Spirit of God to act on behalf of another. London Friends defined this as "a sense of obligation to do something, or to demonstrate sympathetic interest in some individual or group, as a result of what is felt to be a direct intimation of God's will."

Convinced Friend: A member of a meeting who joined after attending a meeting for a period of time. Not a formal process in the early years, committee members visited with those who expressed an interest in joining with the Quakers to determine their sincerity and understanding of the basic tenets. They reported back with their recommendations in the next monthly business meeting, and the membership was usually accepted. The process of deciding to join with the Quakers is known as "convincement."

Deaths: *See Births and Deaths.*

Discipline, Book of: A book outlining the principles of "faith and practice," which are the rules of behavior for Friends as determined by the yearly meeting (the governing body). Among other things, it covered the standards for administration, duties of traveling ministers, and the proper manner of worship. The first printed *Book of Discipline* was published in 1785. Revisions have been made approximately every 20 years since then, with each yearly meeting creating its own from a consensus of the members. (See Chapter 6, "Major Record Types.")

Disownments: The termination of membership that occurred when a member acted contrary to established discipline. A committee was appointed to visit an offender and help him or her to understand how the infraction impacted his or her membership. This process often took several months and was recorded in the minutes. If a member chose not to change, he or she was usually disowned and this action was recorded in the minutes. Conversely, the member could write an apology to the meeting to prevent disownment. Such apologies were also recorded in the minutes. *See Acknowledgements and Apologies.*

Elders: Usually a small group of older men and women who were appointed to assist and oversee the ministers. They opened and closed the meetings for worship in their congregations and gave spiritual guidance, when needed.

Epistles: Formal communications from other meetings. These were generally messages of greeting and usually had more spiritual than informational content.

Financial Records: *See Treasurers under Clerks, Committees, and Other Positions of Responsibility.*

Free Quakers: In 1781, Quakers who supported the American Revolution and were disowned from the main body of the church established their own group called the "Free Quakers." They built a meeting house in 1783, which still stands at the corner of Fifth and Arch streets in Philadelphia. The group disbanded in 1836.

Funerals: *See Memorial Service.*

Gurneyite Friends: Followers of the teachings of English Quaker reformer Joseph John Gurney. This was the common term for members of the larger of the two yearly meetings in New England between 1845 and 1945. Gurneyites were involved in more concentrated evangelical activities and had a "programmed" form of worship, similar to Protestant churches. *See Wilburite Friends.*

Hicksite Quakers: After the Quakers experienced a difficult split in membership in 1827, a large contingency decided to follow the lead of Elias Hicks, a New York Quaker. They were called "Hicksites." They believed in continuing personal revelation and not just in the teachings of the Bible or of traveling ministers. Considered liberal in their thinking, the Hicksites contrasted against a smaller group who called themselves the Orthodox Quakers. You will find records for both the Hicksites and the Orthodox Quakers after the Separation of 1827. Most towns had two Quaker meeting houses, one for each branch, and they each kept separate minute books. *See Orthodox Quakers.*

Indulged Meeting: The name given to a new meeting whose members requested to be considered a formal meeting. It operated under the care of the local monthly meeting until it was decided that the indulged meeting was ready to become a preparative meeting, which was the next step in becoming a monthly meeting.

Inner Light: George Fox taught the early Quakers that there is "that of God in every man," which meant that each person should seek to connect to that "inner light"—the Spirit of God, both in themselves and in others.

Joint Meeting: Men and women initially held their own business meetings and kept their own minutes separately from each other. They began meeting together around the year 1890, so there will be only one set of minutes per meeting after that time.

Laid Down: The term for a meeting that was formally discontinued. Generally, the meeting's membership, assets, and records were transferred to another nearby meeting.

Lay Over: This term referred to postponing a decision. In the Quaker minutes, researchers will find this phrase if a consensus was not reached by the group, leaving the decision until more information was known or until all members had enough time to become comfortable with the decision suggested.

Marriages: The Quakers were given permission to oversee the marriages in their congregations. They considered marriage as one of the most important events in the life of a person and took their responsibility as the governing body very seriously. When a man and woman submitted their marriage intentions to the meeting, a Clearness Committee, usually made up of both men and women, was appointed to investigate the couple's "clearness." They would visit the couple in their own homes, men visiting the groom and women visiting the bride. They usually knew the couple and had watched them grow up. Nevertheless, they wanted to feel confident that the couple understood the sanctity of the marriage vows and the responsibilities they would encounter in marriage and raising a family. The committee reported to the monthly meeting the following month; these reports should appear in the records. Researchers should find items in the minutes referring to the marriage for three consecutive months: the couple's intentions and the assigning of members for the visit should appear in the first month; the committee's report should appear the next month; and the report of the marriage taking place should appear in the third month. If there isn't a completed marriage record in the meeting minutes, the couple may have changed their minds, decided to marry elsewhere, or didn't want to wait and got married by a local priest or magistrate.

Married by a Priest: This term refers to the act of being married by a minister of another religion.

Marriage Certificate: This is a document that was created for the wedding, in which the date of the marriage and the names of the couple, the parents, and the meeting are included. Early

Quaker meeting records usually contain transcripts of marriage certificates and were typically recorded in the home meeting of the bride. After the bride and groom signed their names, family members signed on the right-hand side, directly under the signatures of the bride and groom. Witnesses to the wedding also signed the certificate, and this list of witnesses was also recorded in the minutes. Though these lists are not original signatures, and not all of the witnesses were members, they are often the closest things to membership lists for early meetings. Because the Quakers were responsible for the marriages within their congregations, the marriage certificate took the place of an official document.

Married Contrary to Discipline: A marriage between people who were members of a Quaker meeting but who did not marry under the care of the meeting; for instance, being married by a justice of the peace or a local priest.

Married Out of Unity: A marriage wherein one of the two people was not a member of the Society of Friends.

Meeting for Business: A meeting that discussed the formal affairs of the congregation. Meetings for business could include yearly, quarterly, monthly, or preparative meetings, or committees of any of these. Minutes were usually recorded, in each case.

Meeting for Sufferings: This was a committee created by George Fox to document the abuse of Friends, property that had been confiscated, or other penalties given to Quakers by the English government. These penalties were usually imposed for failure to support the Church of England in tithes and offerings and for not attending church with everyone else. Many Quakers were treated harshly, to the point of imprisonment, for standing up for what they believed. The Meeting for Sufferings administered financial assistance to the families of imprisoned Quakers. They chronicled the sufferings and compiled them into a book written by Quaker Joseph Besse, entitled, "Sufferings of the People Called Quakers." The names of Quakers who suffered are indexed in the back of the book. As the Quakers moved to the New World, a committee with similar financial assistance oversight was created in each meeting, seeing to the needs of Quakers in the Colonies.

Meeting for Worship: This is the name for the Quaker worship service. It was based on the Biblical scripture in Matthew 18:20, "For where two or three have gathered together in my name, there am I in the midst of them." There was no music, no physical communion, and no passing of a collection plate. Members often sat on benches that faced the center and settled into a communal silence, immersed in their own thoughts. If worshippers felt "moved upon by the Holy Ghost" to share something with the other members, they would stand up and speak, which was called "breaking the silence." Sometimes no one stood during the hour. When someone did break the silence and shared a message, generally some time passed before another member broke the silence again, in order to give everyone a chance to consider what was already spoken. It was a great responsibility to break the silence and interrupt the meditation of others; people tended to be very careful about keeping their remarks brief.

Membership Registers: A membership book that contained names of members and dates of births, marriages, and deaths. Not all meetings kept them, and the completeness was often determined by the competence of the recorder. They are more often found after the Separation of 1827.

Memorials: A formal written testimony regarding a deceased member of the Society. Memorials were usually written for more prominent members and were recorded in minute books or separate volumes called "Memorial Books."

Memorial Service: A Quaker funeral service was called a "memorial service" and was usually held in the meeting house. This service for the deceased started as a silent meeting where everyone "settled into silence." *See Meeting for Worship.* A member of the Overseers Committee would break the silence and invite anyone who wanted to share his or her memories of the deceased to stand and speak. The reading of a eulogy was not customary.

Men's Minutes: *See Minutes.*

Ministers: Men and women who were identified as being particularly gifted in speaking the truths and inspired by the Spirit of God. They were formally designated by their monthly meetings and were "recorded" in the minutes. They were not paid but were often supported financially by members of their congregations for their trips. In the early days, it was important that these people be identified because there were people claiming to have the support of their meetings but who were preaching things that were contrary to the tenets of the religion. A minister would often meet with local members during the week to help guide the spiritual life of the meeting they were visiting.

Ministry and Counsel: A committee that cared for the spiritual health of the meeting. Names for this committee with essentially the same function included: Ministry and Oversight; Select Meeting; Ministers and Elders; or Overseers Committee.

Minutes: The formal records of a meeting, written and kept by the Clerk. The information contained in minutes varied widely depending on the date, the meeting, and the clerk. Most minutes contained deliberations on matters like disownments, removals, marriages, meeting houses, creation or dissolution of subordinate meetings, and reports from committees. Before the late 1800s, meetings were held separately for men and women; men's minutes and women's minutes generally covered the same issues, though one or the other might have gone into more detail depending on the discussions. Sometimes an issue that was considered by the women's meeting was sent to the men's meeting for their opinions before any decision was reached. After 1900 or so, most meetings were held jointly with men and women.

Monthly Meeting: The basic unit of administration, which held meetings once a month for business. The monthly meeting held responsibility for recording all of the membership information and is, therefore, the body whose records provide the most historical and genealogical information. They oversaw the care of their members, authorized marriages and removals, considered disciplinary actions, maintained property management, and deliberated over social concerns. Both indulged and preparatory meetings reported up to monthly meetings. Since 1705, monthly meetings have reported up to quarterly meetings, which, in turn, have reported up to yearly meetings. *See Preparatory Meeting.*

Nicolites: A small splinter group of followers of Joseph Nichols, a Quaker from Delaware. They organized as a society in Delaware and along the eastern shore of Maryland in the 1760s. They joined with the Quakers around 1800. Their records are located at the Maryland Hall of Records in Annapolis, MD.

Orthodox Quakers: Members of a branch of Quakers that formed after the Separation of 1827. It was an evangelical group and stressed reliance on the Bible rather than continuing revelation as the authoritative source of religious truths. The Hicksites were the other branch that formed after the Separation of 1827. *See Hicksite Quakers.*

Otisites: This small splinter group of Friends separated themselves from the Wilburites in 1863 and rejoined them in 1911; they were also known as the "Primitive" Quakers.

Overseers: A committee with rotating members selected from the general membership. They were responsible for visiting with members needing discipline, considering marriage, or facing other pressing issues.

Particular Meeting: A small meeting that required oversight from a nearby monthly meeting until it became established.

Preparative Meeting: A single congregation that reported up to a monthly meeting. Most monthly meetings were composed of two or more preparative meetings. An indulged meeting became a preparative meeting as an intermediary step to becoming a monthly meeting. Most preparative meetings eventually became monthly meetings over time or were disbanded.

Primitive Friends: This splinter group of Wilburites formed in Bucks County, PA, in 1860. They wanted to restore the simplicity and discipline found in the writings of the early Quakers.

Quarterly Meeting: An intermediary body between the monthly and yearly meetings, attended by representatives from all monthly meetings. It was generally held four times each year for business. It served as an appellate body for disciplinary matters and considered special problems of interest to all monthly meetings. Quarterly meetings had the authority to establish or discontinue lower-level meetings—monthly, preparative, particular, or indulged.

Queries: A set of questions, posed by a yearly meeting that was querying adherence to standards of behavior as outlined in the *Book of Discipline*. The "responses to queries" by a meeting were usually carefully worded letters reflecting the responses from the members of the congregation.

They are interesting reading, especially those from the early years that discussed Friends' feelings about slavery and the looming Revolutionary War.

Recorded Minister: *See Ministers.*

Removals: *See Certificate of Removal.*

Separation of 1827: The Quakers in Philadelphia split in 1827 and formed two yearly meetings, informally called the "Hicksites" and the "Orthodox." The Hicksites met in the Race Street Meeting House, and the Orthodox met in the Arch Street Meeting House. *See Hicksite Quakers and Orthodox Quakers.*

Sufferings: *See Meeting for Sufferings.*

Testimonies: The basic core practices of the Quakers. Some of the testimonies included: refusal to take oaths, plainness in dress and language, refusal to bear arms (formally referred to as the "Peace Testimony"), refusal to take off hats to social superiors, opposition to slavery, and the equality of men and women.

Traveling Certificate: A document provided to a recorded minister, issued by a meeting, indicating that he or she was allowed to speak for that meeting when visiting or preaching.

Way Will Open: An early Quaker phrase that meant, in general: with patience and time, things will work out for the best.

Wilburite Friends: Followers of the teachings of John Wilbur, a New England Quaker. The common term for members of one of the two yearly meetings in New England, following the split in 1845 and lasting until 1945. Wilburites, sometimes called "Conservative Friends," emphasized the plain life, strict enforcement of discipline, personal revelation, and silent worship. They followed the writings of the early Quakers. *See Gurneyite Friends.*

Women's Meetings: From the earliest years, George Fox encouraged women and men in each congregation to meet separately. He felt that women might be reluctant to speak up in the company of men, and saw their value and inner strength to be equal. *See Minutes.*

Yearly Meeting: The largest gathered body of Quakers, with administrative responsibilities of a general nature. Yearly meetings were made up of representatives from each quarterly meeting and convened once a year for several days to consider weighty matters pertaining to all of their members. They constructed answers to queries from other yearly meetings, formulated discipline, received items of concern from its lower meetings, and generally reviewed the state of the Society within its geographic region.

References and Suggested Reading

1. Berry, David and Ellen. *Our Quaker Ancestors, Finding Them in Quaker Records,* GPC, 1987
2. Eckert, Jack. *Guide to the Records of the Philadelphia Yearly Meeting,* Record Committee of the PYM, 1989
3. Stattler, Richard D. *Guide to the Records of the Religious Society of Friends (Quakers) in New England,* Rhode Island Historical Society, 1997

Major Record Types

CHAPTER 6

Avoid popularity;
it has many snares, and no real benefit.
–William Penn

EARLY QUAKERS WERE ENCOURAGED TO record information about the families and individuals in their congregations. This chapter examines each record type and what to expect to find in them.

Background on Quakers' Record-Keeping Practices

George Fox encouraged Friends to record detailed information about the members of their congregations. As a result, the early Quakers often recorded more information than even the detailed Church of England parish registers. These record-keeping practices of the early Quakers continued when they immigrated to the Colonies. As a result, there are records from the beginning of their establishment in the Colonies, about 1662, which is nearly 200 years prior to the collecting of state vital records.

Membership Records

Membership in the religion was not through a formal application process, at least during the first 50–75 years. Children were considered "Birthright Friends" if their parents were members of a meeting when the children were born. Children who had already been born when their parents decided to join in fellowship with the Quakers were admitted at the request of the parents. Over time, a more formal approach to membership was established, wherein the intent to join with the Quakers was made known to the meeting. You will find an entry to this effect in the meeting minutes, usually with some details about the discussion as well as the date the meeting gave consent. These Quakers were called "Convinced Friends." When an entire family joined the Quakers, all of their names were usually listed in the minutes. Thus, if you find names of your ancestors in the birth register or in the minutes requesting approval for a marriage, a certificate

of removal, or permission for burial, you can assume that they were members even if you do not see a formal request to join the meeting.

Some meetings kept separate "membership registers." In them, you can often find names of at least three generations: a couple's names, their parents' names, and then the names of the children born to them, including when they were born and where. There are often notes in the margins with death dates of the couple and spouses of the children, if known

Monthly Meeting Minutes

The three record books usually kept by meetings were men's meeting minute books, women's meeting minute books, and registers of marriages, births, and burials. Sometimes, separate books of Certificates of Removal, Apologies or Acknowledgements were also kept; these are discussed

---

Figure 6-1: Membership record sample

TIP 1: Membership records are entries about the members of entire family. They usually list the names of the parents, the children's names, and dates of birth

TIP 2: Quite often, the grandparent's names are listed in addition to the parent's names, providing information on another generation. This information is only recorded in this type of record. It is usually not found recorded in the meeting minutes.

WHAT THEY ARE: Membership records are entries about the members of an entire family in a congregation. Membership lists can be family history goldmine because they often list three generations.

WHAT YOU'LL FIND: Names and dates of birth (and sometimes death), as well as family relationships.

GOING FURTHER: If you are given the names of the grandparents, you may be able to find them in the meeting minutes. They will most likely be in the same meeting, or in one nearby.

HINT: There will most likely be a mention recorded in the meeting minutes about the passing of deceased members of the family. Search for these by date. Look for requests for burials as well. Members were usually buried in the burial grounds owned by the meeting. However, keep in mind that in many instances, these records were written when a family moved into the area and joined the meeting. If this is the case, there won't be a mention of the marriage, births (or deaths) in the minutes of this meeting because they didn't occur while the family was under the care of this meeting.

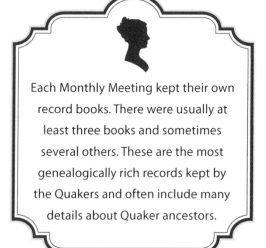

Each Monthly Meeting kept their own record books. There were usually at least three books and sometimes several others. These are the most genealogically rich records kept by the Quakers and often include many details about Quaker ancestors.

The filmed records from monthly meetings in Delaware, Indiana, Maryland, New Jersey, North Carolina, Ohio, Pennsylvania, South Carolina, Tennessee, and Virginia, are now indexed on Ancestry.com. (See Chapter 10, "Resources for Quaker Research—Books, Articles, and Websites," for a list of Quaker repositories with records for states not appearing on this list.)

in other chapters of *Thee and Me*. Many of these books have been microfilmed for preservation purposes, some have been lost, while others still remain with the monthly meeting and have not been preserved. Universities, public libraries, and historical societies also have record books that have been found over the years.

Monthly meeting minutes are from the men's and women's groups which met separately each month to discuss issues that were brought before them from the various preparative meetings. Sometimes, issues considered by the women's meeting were referred to the men's meeting for their consideration. Each group had a scribe, called a "Clerk," who wrote down both the issues and the resolutions. He or she noted announcements, applications, assignments of members from various committees (including their names and the timing of expected reports from them), reports from previous assignments, and any other issues presented at the meeting. It was the clerk's responsibility to not only capture the facts but also the "sense of the meeting," or intent and consensus of feeling and to get approval from the attendees before completing that entry in the minutes.

Monthly meeting minutes are the place to find events such as: births, burials, marriages; requests for certificates of removal; arrivals and departures of members of the congregation; applications for marriage under the care of the meeting; burial requests; and discipline issues. There are no records of baptisms because Quakers did not baptize members. There are also no sacramental records, because Quakers did not perform sacraments. There are no clergy notes, per se, but there are notes from the various committees that took the place of a minister or priest in the pastoral care of the members.

For example, the Worship and Ministry Committee (sometimes called "Ministry and Elders") was a committee that oversaw the spiritual welfare of the meeting and will have reports entered in the minutes. In another example, some records, such as answers to queries from other meetings, traveling certificates, financial accounts, and property records, can be found under "Miscellaneous Papers" in the minute books.

It is always a good idea to comb through all of the records of a monthly meeting. At times, the name you are researching will be in the men's or women's minutes and will not show up in the actual registers for births, marriages, and burials, either because the records were not kept according to instruction or because separate registers of vital records have been lost. Sometimes, younger children were not added to the family list and sometimes, whole families were left off the registers entirely. These omissions were usually the result of human error, not a statement on the

When the Separation of 1827 occurred and the membership split into Orthodox and Hicksite branches, the Hicksite meetings changed the names of some committees, so watch for the new name to start appearing after that date.

membership of that family. Keep in mind, too, that some monthly meetings combined the birth, marriage, and burial records into one book for ease of record keeping. Real people, with real lives, kept the records and they sometimes overlooked details, such as entering data in a timely manner.

When searching the minutes, remember that it is possible that if your ancestor did not move, was not married in that meeting, was not involved in committee work, was not disciplined, did not receive welfare help from the meeting, or married a non-member, his or her name might not surface in the records. These instances are rare but not unheard of. It is still worthwhile to read through the meeting minutes of the meeting where you think your ancestor was a member, just to see what life was like as a Quaker during that time period in that location. You will not only gain a greater understanding of your ancestor's community by reading the minutes, but you will

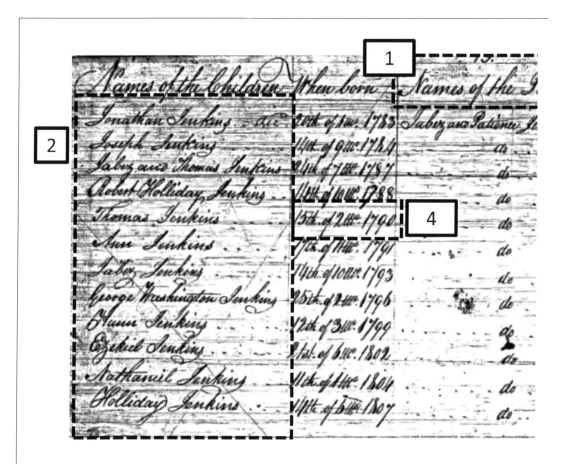

Figure 6-2: Image of birth register

TIP 1: Birth registers identify parents.

TIP 2: Registers sometimes name each child of the family in succession. This usually happens if they are being recorded at a later date.

TIP 3: Registers will often include place of residence.

TIP 4: Quakers numbered months rather than using the common names. So "5 mo. 12 1857" would be "May 12 1857".

TIP 5: Registers will often include comments referring to marriages or deaths of individuals listed.

TIP 6: You may find information about the grandparents.

WHAT IT IS: Records for births of children in

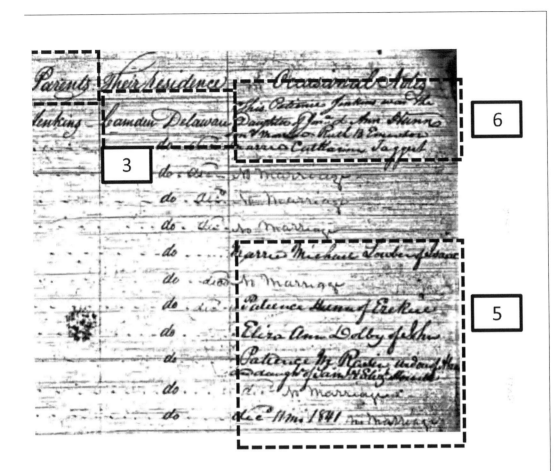

the congregation. Births are sometimes listed by date and sometimes by family group.

WHAT YOU'LL FIND: Names of children, their birth dates and places, and their parent's names.

GOING FURTHER: Quakers started keeping records from their earliest years. Look for the parents in older registers or meeting minutes. You may discover another generation or two!

HINT: Some register books were created long after the births took place. This may have happened because the old book was lost, or in the case of the Separation of 1827, when the Quaker split into two factions, one faction kept the books, and the other had to start over from memory.

see that most of the decisions rendered by the men's and women's meetings were made out of love and concern for their members.

Births

Birthdates were noted in monthly meeting minutes even in the earliest records but especially after 1810, when more meetings began to keep formal register books of births and burials. Births of children born while a family belonged to the meeting were included and sometimes older siblings were entered retrospectively. However, in order to be certain they have located the births of all children of any family, researchers may need to check the records of each monthly meeting to which that family belonged. The Quakers believed in a spiritual christening, without water or a ceremony, so look for birthdates, not for christening or baptismal records.

Quakers in England began keeping register books in 1660. Friends entered their birthdates retrospectively, so some entries go as far back as 1578.

Quaker Marriages and Certificates

You are very fortunate if you find a Quaker marriage certificate for a member of your family. It includes many details about the couple, their parents, and those in attendance at the wedding. A little background about Quaker marriage ceremonies might be helpful in understanding this treasure.

Overview

Quakers had the right, by law, to marry two of their own members starting in 1661. In fact, marriage to a non-Friend under the care of the meeting was not legally possible in England. There are meeting minutes recording thousands of marriages that came "under the care" of the meeting. These marriages were perfectly legal. For more detailed information, read Edward H. Milligan's book on Quaker marriage (*See Selected Bibliography*).

When a couple wanted to be married, the bride and groom approached their meeting for permission to marry. Their requests were recorded in the men's and women's minutes, and two people from the Overseers Committee were appointed to visit the couple individually, men to visit the groom and women to visit the bride. These visits were made to determine if they were each clear to marry—meaning they had no outstanding commitments elsewhere. When the committees reported that both parties were clear, that decision was also noted in the minutes. If the groom was a member of a different monthly meeting, he requested a certificate from his meeting to go to his bride's monthly meeting to marry there. This certificate does not indicate a transfer of membership; it was required in order to show that he was free of all other marriage engagements and was of good character. Without such a certificate, he was not "liberated" to marry the woman by the meeting to which she belonged. After the marriage occurred, the committee reported that the marriage took place. This minute of the accomplished marriage, along with the marriage certificate, become the official records of the event.

Greater Detail

The meeting was responsible for the marriage of the couple on many levels. First, in accordance with local law, the meeting assumed responsibility for keeping careful records of each marriage, thus allowing the meeting to legally prove that a marriage had taken place. *Both the bride and the groom had to be members of the meeting for the marriage to come under the care of the meeting.* The bride and groom were required to appear in person to announce their marriage intentions to the meeting and to request approval from the meeting; they were also required to report their parents' approval of the marriage. A few people were selected from the Committee on Oversight—women to visit the bride and men to visit the groom to discern whether or not they were "free of entanglements." The committee reported back to the monthly meeting the following month, indicating its support or disapproval of the marriage.

Quaker couples who were in a hurry or knew that they would be disowned anyway— for marrying a non-Friend, or a first cousin, or without their parents' consent— often went to a priest to get married. Their marriage dates will not appear in the minutes, but the names of the members would appear when disciplinary action was taken for "marrying contrary to dis-

When recording the marriage of a member of the meeting, if he or she married a non-Quaker, the name of the spouse was not recorded, nor was the location or date of the wedding. So, learning the exact circumstances surrounding a marriage event may not be possible from the meeting minutes.

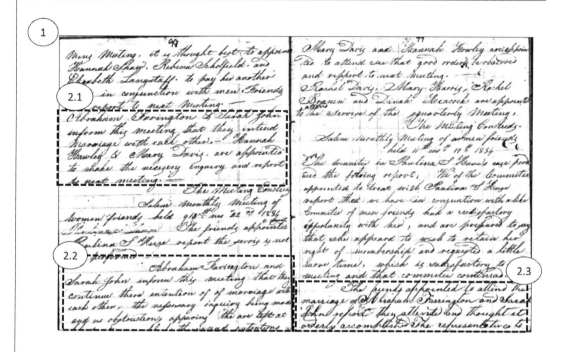

Figure 6-3: Monthly meeting minutes – Marriages

TIP 1: Meeting minutes were kept by both the men's group and the women's group. They usually include different issues that the group discussed. The minutes were kept by the Clerk, a volunteer who is approved by the group. The same person often kept that position for several years.

TIP 2: Meeting minutes will have entries for 3 consecutive months for an upcoming wedding over which the meeting has 'care'.

2.1 Month 1: the bride and groom had to appear before the group and request that

the meeting "oversee" the wedding. Two people are assigned from the "Overseers Committee" or "Committee on Oversight" (you might see either one of these references) to visit with both the groom and bride in their homes and report back; men visiting the groom and women visiting the bride. The appearance by the bride and groom and the names of those assigned to visit with them are recorded in the minutes.

2.2 Month 2: the report from the Overseers is given to the group and recorded in the minutes of the women's meeting. Often the minutes will indicate only that the couple are "cleared for marriage". The two committee members are usually asked by the women's meeting to continue in their assignment and attend the wedding and report back. Sometimes a Date of Liberation certificate was given to the couple, especially if they were going to be married later or elsewhere, indicating the date they were cleared by the meeting to be married.

2.3 Month 3: the third entry will be a report that the wedding was accomplished and the date. In the early years, the entire marriage certificate was copied by the clerk into the minutes, along with the names of all of the attendees who witnessed the marriage ceremony.

WHAT THEY ARE: Records of happenings during the Quaker monthly (business) meeting.

WHAT YOU'LL FIND: Meeting minutes contain a recording of the business conducted in the meeting. This will include declarations of marriage intentions, committee assignments, approvals granted for certificates of removal, weddings, burials, disciplinary actions, and others. Monthly meetings were responsible for all member records, including births, marriages and burials.

GOING FURTHER: A search in the minutes will reveal that couples were sometimes disowned for "marrying out of unity". Quaker couples who were in a hurry, or knew that they would be disowned anyway - for marrying a non-Friend, or a first cousin, or marrying without their parent's consent - would often go to a priest to get married. Their marriage date will not appear in the minutes, but the name of the member will be found when the disciplinary action is taken for "marrying out of unity".

HINT: If a member of the meeting "married out" or married "contrary to discipline" to someone from outside the faith, the name of the spouse was not recorded, nor was the location or date of the wedding. So learning the exact circumstances surrounding an event may not be possible from the meeting minutes.

cipline," or "out of unity", meaning not marrying according to Quaker Discipline. If the non-member spouse wanted to eventually join the meeting, the couple submitted a request to the meeting with an acknowledgement of their infraction.

Research Methodology

There was a definite procedure for Quaker couples to follow when requesting to be married under the care of the meeting. Therefore, a review of the following three steps may help the researcher. These steps usually appeared in the minutes in three consecutive months.

First month: A couple appeared before the meeting to declare their intention to marry and to ask the meeting to oversee the wedding. This step was usually done a few months prior to the planned event. There should be an entry in both the men and women's meeting minutes.

Second month: A committee was appointed, made up of a few members of the congregation. Committee members visited the bride and groom in their respective homes to determine their worthiness to marry. There should be an entry that includes the report given by the committee (usually in the women's meeting minutes) and whether or not permission was granted. The records might also contain an entry sometimes called the "date of liberation," which was the date that the meeting deemed couples to be free to make their wedding plans.

Third month: The third entry should be a report that the wedding was accomplished and on what date. In the early years, the clerk copied the entire marriage certificate into the minutes, along with the names of all of the attendees who witnessed the marriage ceremony. Over time, clerks were no longer required to copy all the names into the minutes.

As already stated, the marriage usually took place under the care of the bride's meeting, either in the meeting house or in her home. There was no clergyman marrying the couple; rather, they offered themselves in marriage and made promises to each other.

The marriage certificate was hand-lettered on large paper, usually velum. As part of the ceremony, the certificate was read aloud to all in attendance as witnesses to the marriage, and all were invited to come forward and sign their names. There was a legal requirement that at least 12 witnesses sign the marriage document; these witnesses could be any members of the meeting. There were several columns of lines where the witnesses signed. It was customary that the bride and groom's family members signed on the right-hand column of the document, under the names of the bride and groom, usually with parents' names first. Then the rest of the attendees—whether old or young—signed their names to the certificate as legal witnesses to the ceremony. Anyone could attend the wedding, so researchers cannot assume that the names found on the certificate were all Quakers. However, finding a list of all the witnesses in the meeting minutes can be a true genealogical treasure. Quakers attended many weddings as a show of support, so it is valuable to read the names from marriage records in the meeting where your ancestor attended.

You may be wondering what happened if the committee found that it could not approve of the marriage taking place under the care of the meeting. When this occurred, the couple usually found a civil magistrate to marry them. After some time had passed, the couple's names may show up in the minutes when they submitted an apology for "marrying out of discipline." They were usually accepted back into the fold.

Some of the reasons for refusing a request to be married under the care of the meeting are probably what you would expect. They include:

- Marrying someone not of his or her faith and who had no intention of joining

- Parental objections

- Marrying someone who had been engaged to marry another and recently broke that engagement, thus requiring more time for inquiry

A family Bible or other record may show that a couple was married in a certain meeting house. The meeting house was owned by a Meeting for Worship, and the Preparative Meeting may have reported to different monthly meetings over the years. Researchers must determine which monthly meeting it reported to on the date that the wedding took place and search for the marriage certificate in that monthly meeting's records. The best place to locate information on the changes Preparative Meetings made in reporting is on QuakerMeetings.com. See Chapter 10, "Resources for Quaker Research" for more information about this website.

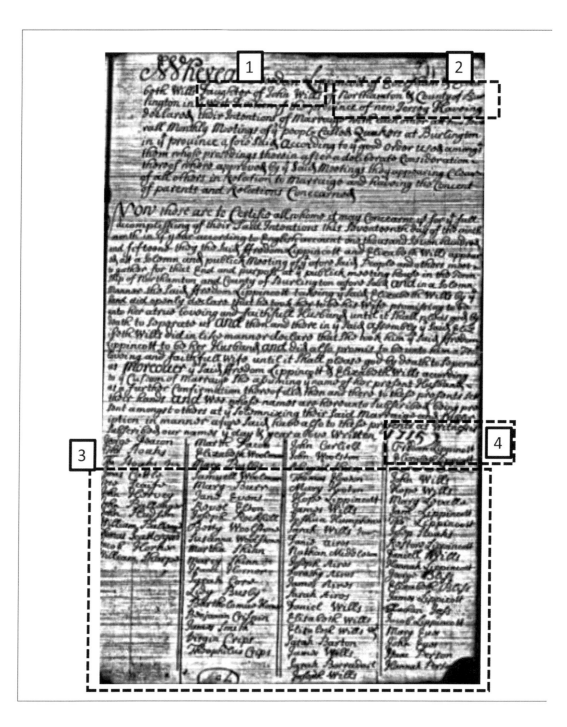

Figure 6-4: Quaker Marriage Certificate

TIP 1: Marriage records usually include names of parents of both bride and groom, and whether or not they are living or deceased.

TIP 2: Marriage records will indicate where the bride and groom are from and often where their parents are from.

TIP 3: All attendees to the wedding are witnesses and sign the marriage certificate as legal witnesses that the 1marriage took place.

TIP 4: Here you will the signatures of the bride and groom and usually the date.

WHAT IT IS: A Quaker marriage certificate is a legal document. It takes the place of a civil document and is proof that the wedding took place. Quakers were given a special legal dispensations in England and America to marry their own. In the early days, meetings could oversee marriages only when the bride and groom were both members of that meeting (congregation) and where the meeting had entered the details into the minutes – as proof that it took place. All the people in attendance are legal witnesses and sign their names as such.

WHAT YOU'LL FIND: Among the signatures, look for names of family members, relatives visiting for the wedding, prominent Quakers and even children.

GOING FURTHER: Marriage certificates become treasured heirlooms in Quaker families and are often passed down through the generations. There are many to be found in the Quaker Collection on Ancestry. Keep in mind that these are not the originals. They were copied into the minutes by the clerk of the meeting. After a while, they stopped including the names of the witnesses because it wasn't required by law, and because it was laborious work.

- Pregnancy

- First cousins who wished to marry (approved in some states, but not by the Quakers)

Widowers and widows were usually required to wait at least one year after the death of a spouse to remarry, although this time requirement varied over the years. With the high number of deaths during childbirth, the waiting period was often reduced so that a man could quickly find a new wife to mother his small children.

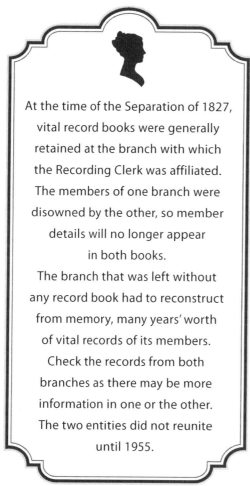

At the time of the Separation of 1827, vital record books were generally retained at the branch with which the Recording Clerk was affiliated. The members of one branch were disowned by the other, so member details will no longer appear in both books.

The branch that was left without any record book had to reconstruct from memory, many years' worth of vital records of its members. Check the records from both branches as there may be more information in one or the other. The two entities did not reunite until 1955.

Deaths and Burial Records

London Friends created their own burying grounds on their property out of necessity, as they were not permitted to be buried in parish graveyards. American Friends continued this practice and burial grounds were usually created on property adjoining the meeting house; they were often protected by simple stone walls.

Burial records vary by monthly meeting. There will often be a mention of a member's passing in the meeting minutes and the circumstances were sometimes recorded, but not always and especially not if there was a suicide or murder involved. The date of death may have been recorded in the membership records, especially if the person died at a young age. You may also see a note about it in the margin of the meeting minutes. Some meetings kept separate burial or death register books. (See Chapter 12, "Meeting Houses and Quaker Burial Grounds," for more information about Quaker deaths and burials.)

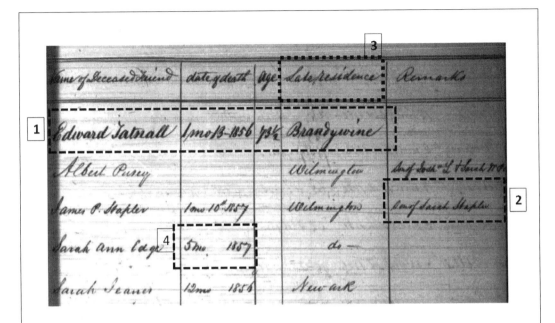

Figure 6-5: Death Registers

TIP 1: Death registers identify the name of the deceased, the date of death, the age if know, and the place of residence

TIP 2: They sometimes name the parents, if known.

TIP 3: the term "Late Residence" was a term used in the 18th & 19th century meaning the deceased's most recent residence

TIP 4: Quakers numbered months rather than using the common names. So "5 mo. 12 1857" would be "May 12 1857".

WHAT IT IS: Registers (books) with list of deaths of members of the congregation.

WHAT YOU'LL FIND: Names of the deceased, the date they died, age of the deceased, and place of residence.

GOING FURTHER: Look for a note in the meeting minutes about the passing of the deceased; usually somewhere near the date you see in the Death Register. There are often details recorded there regarding the cause of death, especially if there was a protracted illness.

HINT: You may also find a note in the meeting minutes regarding permission being requested (and granted) for burial in the meeting burial grounds.

Another source of death dates is entitled *Memorials of Deceased Friends*. These were books written by several yearly meetings and containing short entries about many Quakers. There have been several manuscripts of these memorials printed. One example is entitled, *Quaker Biographical Sketches of Ministers and Elders, and other Concerned Members of the Yearly Meeting of Philadelphia, 1682-1800.*

Here is a sample memorial from that book (page 126):

> ## ISAAC WILLIAMS.
>
> Isaac Williams received a gift of gospel ministry, whilst a member of Gwynnedd Monthly Meeting, and was diligent in the performance of his religious duties. About the beginning of the year 1735, he removed to Middletown Meeting, Bucks county, taking with him a certificate of the full unity of Friends of Gwynnedd with his ministry. Middletown Friends say of him: "During his short residence amongst us, he approved himself a man of sobriety and orderly life and conversation, a diligent attender of meetings, and in the ministry lively and edifying." His decease took place about the close of the Seventh month, 1735.

TEXT FROM IMAGE:

Isaac Williams

Isaac Williams received a gift of gospel ministry whilst a member of Gwynnedd Monthly Meeting {Pennsylvania}, and was diligent in the performance of his religious duties. About the beginning of the year 1735, he removed to Middletown Meeting, Bucks County, taking with him a certificate of the full unity of Friends of Gwynnedd with his ministry. Middletown Friends say of him: "During his short residence amongst us, he approved himself a man of sobriety and orderly life and conversation, a diligent attender of meetings, and in the ministry lively and edifying." His decease took place about the close of the Seventh month, 1735.

Memorials varied in length and may not include many genealogical details but notice that the names of two monthly meetings are mentioned: Gwynnedd and Middletown. Clues like these can help to further the research on Isaac Williams and his family, as the minutes of those two meetings are consulted.

References and Suggested Reading

1. 1717 Quaker *Book of Discipline*
2. Austin, Mary E. *Courtship and Marriage of Ye Old Time Quakers.* New Bedford, Mass.: Old Dartmouth Historical Society, 1912 [Book on Ancestry.com]
3. Baldwin, Steven. http://www.rootsweb.com/~quakers/sb.htm
4. Comfort, William Wistar. Quaker Marriage Certificates, *The Bulletin of Friends Historical Association,* (Autumn 1951) :40-2
5. http://www.qhpress.org/texts/obod/births.html

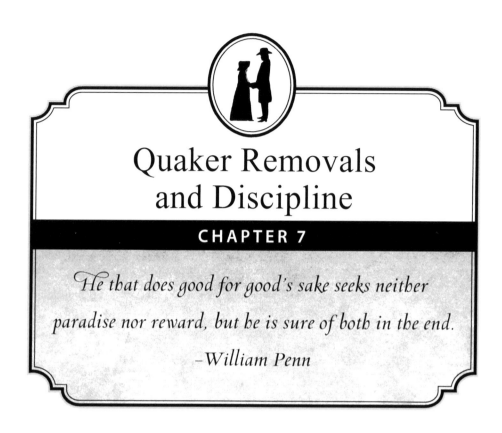

Quaker Removals and Discipline

CHAPTER 7

He that does good for good's sake seeks neither paradise nor reward, but he is sure of both in the end.

–William Penn

CERTIFICATES OF REMOVAL (REMOVAL IS an English term meaning "to relocate") are often essential sources of information for research. The process of moving from meeting to meeting provided documents that can help to track the migration of Quaker ancestors. However, few records cause researchers as much confusion as the disciplinary actions of Quaker meetings. This chapter outlines the concepts behind both of these record types and how they affect research.

Certificates of Removal

When a family or individual wished to move to a locality that was within the boundaries of another meeting, regardless of the distance, they were required by the Book of Discipline to request and receive a certificate of removal in order to transfer their membership. This could be considered a letter of reference from the original meeting. The normal procedure involved a review by a few members of the Committee of Overseers, who were appointed to determine if there were any unmet financial obligations or other serious issues. After the review, a certificate was prepared, indicating that the individuals or families were members in good standing and no "obstruction" was found. The purpose of this document was to assure the new meeting that the persons arriving were of sound stature and had fulfilled their obligations. If an obstruction was found, the certificate was withheld until the obstruction was cleared up. When you consider the circumstances of traveling over long distances and sometimes even oceans, with no means of knowing whether or not the arriving people were trustworthy, it is not difficult to understand the need of such a document. With this letter or certificate, the new individual or family was welcomed to the meeting. It was a fairly reliable way of keeping the congregation safe from being taken advantage of by unscrupulous people.

The certificate was for the adults and their minor children and usually listed them by name. The older children were listed on their own certificates, though there was no hard rule about it. In some instances, as in the case of mass migration, several families were included on one certificate.

The information contained in the certificate was written into the minutes of the former meeting, and when the certificate holders reached their destination, the information was written into the minutes of the new meeting (though this didn't become a general practice until the mid-1700s). After that time, it is possible to track families through their migrations using their Certificates of Removal. You can often gauge how long it took them to travel to their new homes by tracking the time, starting with the month a certificate was read into the former

If a disowned member moved to attend another meeting and sought approval for marriage, he or she was required to obtain a certificate from his or her former meeting. A formal written apology was required and will be in the minutes. After the member's reinstatement, the disowning meeting usually sent a Certificate of Removal to the new meeting. This may be confusing to researchers because the certificate date in the minutes will not correlate with the original disownment date, in fact it may appear in the minutes years after the disownment. (see "Disciplinary Actions—Disownments and Apologies" later in this chapter).

meeting minutes and ending with the month a certificate was read into the new meeting minutes. Eventually, these certificates were sent directly to the new meetings, not carried by the families.

The system was not perfect, and you may find a record of a Certificate of Removal in the former meeting's minutes and then not find a record of the certificate in the minutes of the intended meeting. There could have been several reasons for this occurrence: perhaps the certificate was

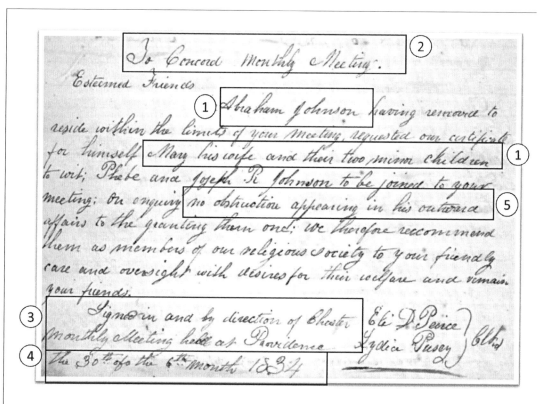

Figure 7-1: Certificate of Removal

TIP 1: Look for names and family relationships.

TIP 2: The certificate is addressed to the new meeting, indicating the destination for this family.

TIP 3: The certificate is issued by the current meeting, where the family or individual is moving from.

TIP 4: The date provides a time frame for the move.

lost; perhaps the travelers changed their plans; or, as often happened, their plans were changed for them (for example, through loss of life or finances) while traveling to their new location. In that case, research collateral lines to determine where other family members lived and locate the Quaker meeting closest to that area. If there were no Quaker meetings in the vicinity, they may have joined another church.

TIP 5: The phrase "no obstruction appearing in his outward affairs" refers to the general financial condition of the family or individual.

WHAT IT IS: A letter of transit for a person or family who is leaving one meeting and moving to another. The main purpose of this document was to assure the new meeting that the persons arriving could be trusted and that their meeting knew the family well enough to be able to vouch for them. With this letter or certificate, a new family or person would be welcomed immediately to the meeting, and given any needed assistance in order to get settled.

WHAT YOU'LL FIND: The names of the current and destination meetings, a date, and the name of the individual or family moving. A family certificate will list the husband, and usually the names of the wife and minor children. Older children will have their own certificate. A certificate of removal will always include a statement about the general financial welfare of the departing individual or family.

GOING FURTHER: The information contained in the certificate of removal was written into the minutes of the former meeting when parties left. When they reached their destination, it was entered into the minutes of the new meeting, though not all meetings conformed to this practice at first. After about the mid-1700s, it is possible to track a family through their meetings by reading their certificates of removal.

HINT: Removal Registers, separate books tracing the requests for certificates and the approvals given, were kept by many meetings. In other meetings, the requests and approvals are found only in the body of the minutes. Check for both possibilities by using the "Browse" function in the Meeting Minutes for the meeting where your ancestor lived. This will show you a list of all the record types for that meeting in this database. If there is no Register of Removals, then check the meeting minutes directly.

Finding Certificates of Removal in the Records

Removal registers, separate books that traced the removal requests and approvals, were kept by many meetings. In other meetings, the requests and approvals are found only in the minutes. Use the Browse function on Ancestry.com in the *U.S., Quaker Meeting Records, 1681–1994*, or the *England and Wales, Quaker Birth, Marriage, and Death Registers, 1578–1837* to locate the meeting where your ancestor lived and to view a list of all the records for that meeting. If there is no book entitled "Register of Removals", then check the meeting minutes directly.

As you move backward through the generations in your family tree to the earliest Colonial years and then back to Great Britain, pay particular attention to the places mentioned in the records you find. A Certificate of Removal will mention the names of both the current and future meetings but not usually the town names. On the other hand, a will or a land record usually indicates the town and county but not which meeting a member attended. Because meeting names can be quite similar, you will need all of these facts in order to determine which county they lived in and the name of the meeting they attended.

Disciplinary Actions—Disownments and Apologies

Few things in early Quaker records confuse new researchers as much as the disciplinary actions that meetings took toward individuals. Some people today apply current standards of behavior and connotations of words to the actions and activities of Quakers 300 years ago. Be mindful of this, and instead of tending toward judgment, try to see the bigger picture of what they were trying to accomplish.

General Discipline Guidelines

Each yearly meeting produced its own *Book of Discipline*. It was patterned after the work of George Fox and closely followed his teachings. All Quakers knew of the Disciplines because they were openly discussed in meetings. The early Friends were a people who were encouraged by their leaders to live as Christ lived, using patterns of behavior that others could emulate. It was a high ideal, but it was what they strove to do, daily. They tried to live in quietism, relying on the whisperings of the Holy Spirit to guide their lives. If there were members who could not or would not live in accordance with the established and accepted patterns of behavior and could not be persuaded to change their behavior, then Friends did what they could to distance themselves from those individuals. By disowning them, they were declaring that the meeting would not "own" their *behaviors*; these behaviors were disowned. But disownments did not happen hastily. "No Friend was ever disowned by surprise" was a common phrase; it meant that the individual was counseled many times and given every opportunity to change his or her ways before the meeting decided to disown him or her. They were encouraged to continue attending meeting and staying close to the community. This was the way Quakers found to "love the sinner and hate the sin."

Friends were counseled to handle the infractions and the discipline with love:

Philadelphia Book of Discipline, 1807:

"It is advised, that where any transgress the rules of our discipline, they may, without partiality, be admonished and sought in the spirit of love and divine charity, so that it may be seen by all that the restoring spirit of meekness and Christian love abounds, before church censure takes place, and that a gospel spirit is the spring and motive to all our performances, as well in discipline as in worship.

It is earnestly recommended, that in conducting the affairs of the church, Friends endeavor {sic} to manage them in the peaceable spirit and wisdom of Jesus, with decency, forbearance and love to each other."

Both the infraction and the discipline were noted in the minutes:

If a member went against the Disciplines, it was noted in the minutes along with the names of members who were assigned to visit with the individual about his or her conduct. If the member felt remorse, he or she could write a letter of apology or acknowledgement to the meeting, requesting forgiveness for the infraction. If the member did not feel regret and planned to continue in his or her activities, this intention was reported back to the meeting, and disownment was usually the eventual outcome. Both the visit and the decision were recorded in the minutes. Being disowned was not the same as shunning or excommunication, as were common in other religions; it simply meant that they could not attend the business meetings and vote. This distinction was significant because all members of the meeting were encouraged to attend business meetings and contribute their opinions, both men and women. Additionally, those who were disowned could not be of service by serving on committees, and any children born to the family were not birthright Quakers. Researchers should take note that names of disowned members were no longer mentioned in the minutes. This point remained the case until and unless they requested to be reinstated and wrote a letter of apology to the meeting. Apologizing tended to be more common if they wanted to move to another meeting and needed a Certificate of Removal. It was less common if the member married someone who was not a Quaker.

In your research, you will notice books kept by the meetings entitled, *Books of Apologies* or just, *Acknowledgments*. These are books of letters from members who desired to return to the meeting; in them are written apologies where they are acknowledging their mistakes and asking to be reinstated. The Quakers believed that the Disciplines were standards that any Christian would and should follow. They therefore expected the same of any members who professed to be Quakers and presented themselves to the community as such.

When a member was disowned, if he or she felt that the decision was made in error, the Book of Discipline provided for an appeal process which operated much the same as a lawsuit appeal, moving to ever higher courts. The disowned member was permitted to make an appeal to the quarterly meeting to which the monthly meeting belonged. If the disowned member was not satisfied with the resulting decision, he or she could appeal to the yearly meeting for a final decision.

Disownment rules changed gradually beginning in about 1850 among different groups of Friends. By the 1890s, only a few more traditional groups still made it an offense to marry outside the faith and instead reserved this action for offences such as theft or adultery. By about 1900, the practice of disownment was stopped altogether.

Here is a partial list of offenses that would most likely have led to an early Quaker being disowned:

- Drinking to excess
- Being habitually absent from meeting
- Marrying a first cousin
- Marrying without parental consent
- Marrying a non-Quaker (Friends strongly believed in religious unity within the family.)
- Stealing or any type of lying; theft or any dishonesty, including bankruptcy
- Parenting an illegitimate child
- Committing adultery
- Paying tithes to the Anglican (and eventually any) church

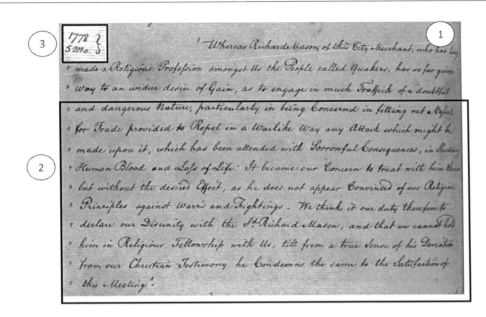

Figure 7-2: Disownments and Apologies

TIP 1: Disciplinary actions were formal procedures wherein an offender was counseled in private by a small group of Friends about offending behavior. If they were not willing to apologize, they were "disowned". This enabled Quakers to continue to love the "sinner" but hate the "sin". The offender was not ostracized but was encouraged to come to meeting, although he/she was not allowed to voice opinions in the business meeting. The act of disownment was a serious matter to Friends, not taken without cause or without a good deal of discussion. A summary of the discussions will appear in the meeting minutes.

TIP 2: Some of the offences for which early Quakers were disowned were in alignment with their basic tenets. Quakers believed that war and aggression were not the Lord's way of solving any problem. Quakers who went to war, or carried a weapon, or helped with war efforts (making wheel rims or bullets), was acting against the Friend's " Peace Testimony" and were open to disownment as a result of their actions.

TIP 3: Look for a date in the upper corner of the page. Or it may imbedded in the text. Quakers numbered months rather than using the common names. So "5 mo. 1778" would be "May 1778".

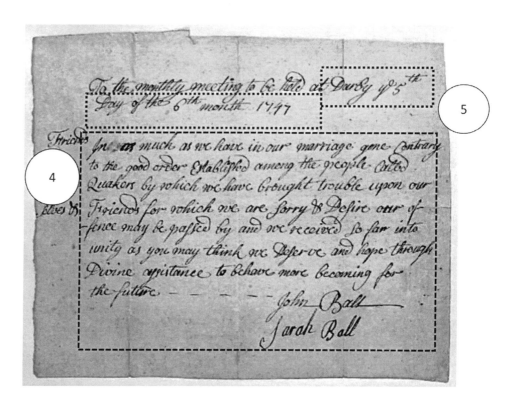

TIP 4: If the offending Friend repented, he/she was asked to write a letter of apology to the meeting acknowledging that the misdeeds were offensive to Friend's principles and discipline. These records are called "Apologies" or "Acknowledgements" and will appear either in the minutes or in separate books.

TIP 5: Meeting name and date are usually included. Quakers numbered months rather than using the common names; and didn't change from the Julian to the Gregorian calendar until 1752. So "5th day of 6th mo. 1747" would be "July 5 1747".

WHAT THEY ARE: Disciplinary action were taken on occasion in an effort to define and reinforce the basic tenets of the religion. These included disownments, in which a meeting affirmed that it did not "own" nor take responsibility for the behavior of the offender. "Apologies" and "Acknowledgments" are formal statements written to the congregation apologizing for offending behavior.

WHAT DETAILS YOU'LL FIND: Details about the offence are sometimes included in the written statement. The details will not be found in the Hinshaw Encyclopedia because the individuals doing the abridgements were asked to keep all such details out of the Hinshaw notes. The offence will be found in the meeting minutes although the extent of the details will vary according to the discretion of the clerk keeping the records.

GOING FURTHER: Sometimes meetings worked for years with offenders, resulting in multiple entries in the minutes. It is worth the time to read through all of them in order to get an accurate picture. A disownment was never final, although the passing of a year or more was the norm before an offender could apply for reinstatement. Disownments were phased out in the late 1800s.

HINT: Quakers could face disownment for numerous reasons. These include: theft, marrying a non-Quaker, public intoxication, gambling, and others.

- Being directly or indirectly involved with any war effort

References and Suggested Reading

1. Hinshaw, William Wade, *Encyclopedia of American Quaker Genealogy, Vol V.*

Hinshaw Collections — Published and Unpublished

CHAPTER 8

*Speak properly, and in as few words as you can,
but always plainly; for the end of speech is not ostentation,
but to be understood.*

–William Penn

YOU MAY HAVE HEARD OF a collection called "Hinshaw" or the "Encyclopedia of American Quaker Genealogy." You may have even tried to use this resource to locate your Quaker ancestor and ended up confused by the abbreviations. This chapter discusses the Hinshaw collections, both the published and unpublished, and gives researchers important clues concerning this large body of work including the abbreviations created especially for each volume. A case study is included, illustrating how best to apply the collections to Quaker research.

William Wade Hinshaw

W.W. Hinshaw (1867–1947) was raised by Quaker parents in Union, IA. He rose to fame in the music world, enjoying a career in the world of opera, touring the United States and Canada, performing in concerts from 1890 to 1918. At one point, he was the leading baritone at the Metropolitan Opera Company in New York.

Hinshaw devoted the final 20 years of his life to gathering and compiling Quaker records that contained detailed and important genealogical data before they were lost, destroyed, or decayed. Hinshaw's plan was to collect and compile the data from the thousands of Quaker records in existence and make the data accessible to the hundreds of thousands of Quaker descendants. Sadly, he did not live to see this work completed. At his passing, Hinshaw's wife gave the entire collection of thousands of type-written index cards (which were to be assembled into many more volumes) to Swarthmore College Friends Historical Library. The collection is housed in a card file that covers a 20-foot-long wall in the small library.

Both of Hinshaw's works, the encyclopedia and the Unpublished Index Cards, are part of the Quaker Collection at Ancestry.com.

Hinshaw's *Encyclopedia of American Quaker Genealogy* (EAQG)

Hinshaw's original vision was to include all the monthly meetings of North America in this EAQG, which didn't happen for several reasons. First, he ran into difficulty locating all the records. As a result, he decided to concentrate his efforts on getting the records from areas of the United States where he felt genealogy material was not readily available. He therefore did not attempt to get any records from the New England area. Second, Hinshaw could not get permission to have the records moved to a central location, so he was forced to hire people who were able to travel to wherever the records were located, in order to perform the work. Extracted details were to be placed on index cards and alphabetized by surname in preparation for printing, a laborious task prior to the invention of the computer. The third reason that he did not realize his dream was the resistance he found within the Religious Society of Friends. The yearly meetings decided they did not want the issues of the lives of the early Quakers exposed for scrutiny. They insisted that Hinshaw's teams remove private details. This element added more time to the project, besides creating challenges for today's researchers. Hinshaw's collection did not include all recorded details of the meeting records, so it should be considered an abridgment and not an abstraction. Records in the Hinshaw volumes have been taken out of context and placed in alphabetical order by surname; then in chronological order. The Hinshaw team faced a major challenge in working with the Quaker records; many of the families had either identical or very similar names, making it very difficult to pinpoint the families to which some individuals belonged.

The result is a six-volume set of books published between 1936 and 1950, extracted from early Quaker records kept since Colonial years. Commonly called "Hinshaw" or "Hinshaw's Encyclopedia," it was the largest index of names from Quaker meeting minutes until Ancestry. com put the original Quaker records online.

Important points to remember about the Hinshaw books:

- With many of the details "scrubbed" at the request of yearly meetings, researchers must read the original minutes to find more context.

- *Hinshaw's collection is not a list of all Quakers in the United States.* Hinshaw was only able to publish six volumes prior to his death. These six volumes contain only a fraction of the total meetings.

- The "Unpublished Hinshaw Index Cards" contain nearly 900,000 names, but according to the Friends Historical Library at Swarthmore College, *the majority of Friends' meeting minutes were never abstracted* and will not be found in either of the Hinshaw collections.

U.S., Hinshaw's Index to Unpublished Quaker Records, 1640-1930

The index contains records that were extracted from the minutes of 300 meetings from the East Coast to Nebraska. (See a list of meetings on the collection home page). These meetings are <u>not</u> included in the published volumes called the "Encyclopedia of American Quaker Genealogy". They are primarily from meetings in Indiana (86 meetings), Iowa (84 meetings), Kansas (49 meetings), Pennsylvania (13 meetings), and New Jersey (4 meetings). There are also extracts from a few meetings in the following states: Arizona, California, Colorado, Idaho, Illinois, Michigan, Minnesota, Missouri, Nebraska, Oklahoma, South Dakota, and Wisconsin. If you do not find your ancestor's meeting in this collection, you will need to consult the original minutes for that meeting, because they were not included in the project.

There is a list of abbreviations used in the extraction of the records. It is an essential tool for pulling all of the research hints from the cards you find. Print a copy and keep it handy!

U.S., Surname Index to Quaker Records

This database contains a cross-index to *Hinshaw's Index to Selected Quaker Records, 1640-1940*. It is a list of surnames found in Hinshaw's Index, and each name is followed by a list of meetings in which that surname appears in the collection. This database has not been indexed, but names are listed in alphabetical order. Hinshaw's teams were only able to complete the work of extracting meeting minutes for 300 meetings in 17 states, and there have been close to 2000 meetings. You may find that it is worthwhile checking the list to see where your ancestor's surname appears; it may offer just the clue you need to continue your research.

```
LINTON:    California - Whittier; Colorado - Colorado Springs; Indiana
   Coloma, Greenwood, Hopewell Vermilion County, Indianapolis, La
   Porte, Marion, Providence, Sugar River; Michigan - Detroit; Ne-
   braska - Plainview, Spring Bank; New Jersey - Woodbury; Pennsyl-
   vania - Chester, Frankford, Goshen, London Grove, New Garden,
   Philadelphia Northern District, Philadelphia Southern District,
   Stroudsburg.
LINTT:    Nebraska - Plainview.
LINVILLE, LINDVILLE, LINWILL, etc.:    Indiana - Greentown, Knights-
   town, Marion, New Salem, South Marion, Spiceland; New Jersey -
   Haddonfield; Pennsylvania - Exeter, Kennett, New Garden.
LINUS:    Pennsylvania - New Garden.
LIONHARDT:    Iowa - Bloomington, Springdale.
LIONORI:    Iowa - Chestnut Hill.
LIOSEY:    Iowa - Lynnville.
LIPPERT:    Iowa - Albia, Des Moines.
LIPPINCOTT, LIPPENCOTT:    Iowa - Le Grand; New Jersey - Evesham, Had-
   donfield, Mt. Holly, Woodbury; Pennsylvania - Chester, Chester
   Hicksite, Concord, Darby Hicksite, Frankford, Goshen, Gwynedd,
   Muncy, New Garden, Philadelphia Northern District, Philadelphia
   Southern District.
LIPPLE:    Kansas - Mt. Tabor.
LIPSEY, LIPSY:    Indiana - Back Creek, Blue River, Indianapolis,
   Knightstown, Marion, Plainfield, Sand Creek; Iowa - Ackworth,
   Coal Creek Conservative, Motor,
LISBY:    Indiana - Amo, Mill Creek.
LISCOMB, LISCOME, LIPSCOMB(E):    Indiana - South Wabash, Wabash;
   Iowa - Albion, Marshalltown.
```

FIGURE 8-1: This list of almost 100 abbreviationsis used throughout all six volumes of the Encyclopedia of American Quaker Genealogy. Most volumes also have specific abbreviation codes for their meetings and burial grounds. See those codes listed under each volume.

Abbreviations Used

The Hinshaw teams developed a set of abbreviations that are used in all six volumes. Each abbreviation is used to represent a word, several words, or an entire sentence, which are found in all meeting minutes and have been commonly used by meeting clerks for over 300 years. These abbreviations were created in order to save space, time and cost; but it takes time to get accustomed to using them.

Keep this list nearby to expand the abbreviations you find in the Hinshaw encyclopedia records.

FIGURE 8-2: Hinshaw Abbreviation Chart

For explanations - see Chapter 5: Glossary of Early Quaker Terms

Abbreviation	Expanded Text
acc	accept; accepted; acceptable
ack mo	acknowledged marriage out
alto	at liberty to marry
ami	announced marriage intentions
amist	announced marriage intentions second time
att	attached to; attended
b	born
BG	Burial Grounds
bur	buried; burial
c.	circa (about)
cd	contrary to discipline
cert	certificate
ch	child; children
chr	charter
clear	clear with respect to marriage
co	chosen overseer
com	complained; complained of
comm	committee
con	condemned
d	died
dec	deceased
dis	disowned; disowned for

Abbreviation	Expanded Text
div	divorced
dmi	declared marriage intentions
dmist	declared marriage intentions second time
dp	dropped plain dress and/or speech
dr	drinking spirituous liquor to excess
dt	daughter; daughters
dtd	dated
end	endorsed
exms	excused from military service
fam	family
FBG	Friends Burial Ground
form	former; formerly
Frds	Friends
gc	granted certificate
gct	granted certificate to
gc efms	granted certificate excusing from military service
gl	granted letter
h	husband
jas	joined another society
jG	joined Gurneyites
jH	joined Hicksites
jO	joined Orthodox

Abbreviation	Expanded Text
JP	Justice of the Peace
jW	joined Wilburites
ltm	liberated to marry or left at liberty to marry
m	marry; married; marrying; marriage
ma	marriage authorized
mbr	member
mbrp	membership
mcd	married contrary to discipline
MG	Minister of the Gospel
MH	meeting house, church
MM	monthly meeting
mos	married out of society
mou	married out of unity
mtg	meeting
neg att	neglecting attendance
ni	not identified
nm	non member
nmtm	not a member of this meeting
ou	out of unity
PM	particular or preparative meeting
prc	produced certificate
prcf	produced certificate from
prlf	produced letter from
QM	quarterly meeting
rcd	recorded
rec	received; recommended
recrq	received by request

Abbreviation	Expanded Text
relrq	released by request
rem	remove; removed
rem cert	removal certificate
ret mmbrp	retained membership
rm	reported married
rmt	reported married to
roc	received on certificate
rocf	received on certificate from
rcl	received on letter
rclf	received on letter from
rpd	reported
rq	request; requests; requested
rqc	requested certificate
rqct	requested certificate to
rqcuc	requested to come under care (of meeting)
rqlt	requested letter to
rst	reinstate; reinstated
rtco	referred to care of
s	son; sons
twp	township
uc	under care (of meeting)
unm	unmarried
upl	using profane language
w	wife
w/c	with consent of
wd	widow
YM	Yearly Meeting

Encyclopedia of American Quaker Genealogy –
A Brief Description of each of the Six Volumes

Volume I

Volume I was published in 1936. The title page indicates that it contains abstracts from the "Records and Minutes of the Thirty-Three Oldest Monthly Meetings" in North Carolina. It also includes abstracts from the early records of Tennessee, South Carolina, Georgia, and one meeting in Virginia. The foreword and introduction give valuable information as to which meetings and what information was abstracted. This explanation from the Friends Historical Collection at Guilford College helps in understanding the arrangement of the abstractions:

Each meeting is introduced with a brief history that includes the names of the earliest members. Next is a section listing information from the meeting's birth and death records, arranged alphabetically by family surname. The third section is an abstract of the minutes of the meeting, including marriages, new memberships, transfers of membership, disownments, and restorations of membership. Entries for each meeting are arranged alphabetically by family, and then chronologically."

Vol. I contains the following meetings (note that "MM" stands for "Monthly Meeting"):

Georgia
- Wrightsborough MM, GA

North Carolina
- Back Creek MM, NC
- Cane Creek MM, NC
- Center MM, NC
- Contentnea (Nahunta) MM, NC
- Core Sound MM, NC
- Deep Creek MM, NC
- Deep River MM, NC
- Dover MM, NC
- Greensboro MM, NC
- High Point MM, NC
- Holly Spring MM, NC
- Hopewell MM, NC
- Marlborough MM, NC
- Neuse MM, NC
- New Garden MM, NC
- Pasquotank (Symons Creek) MM, NC
- Perquimans (Piney Woods) MM, NC
- Rich Square MM, NC (incl. Jack Swamp)
- Spring MM, NC
- Springfield MM, NC
- Suttons Creek MM, NC
- Union MM, NC
- Westfield MM, NC
- Woodland MM, NC

Tennessee

- Lost Creek MM, TN
- New Hope MM, TN
- Newberry (Friendsville) MM, TN

South Carolina

- Bush River MM, SC
- Cane Creek MM, SC
- Charleston MM, SC
- Piney Grove MM, SC

Virginia

- Mt. Pleasant (Chestnut Creek) MM, VA

Volume II

Volume II was published in 1938. It contains abridgments for "Four of the Oldest Monthly Meetings" of the Philadelphia Yearly Meeting of Friends. In his introduction to this volume, Hinshaw states that the yearly meeting is perhaps better described by the title that it sometimes used: *The Yearly Meeting of Pennsylvania, New Jersey, Delaware, and part of Maryland and Virginia.* While it was neither the first nor always the largest yearly meeting of Friends in America, Philadelphia Yearly Meeting has long been considered the epicenter of Quakerism on this continent.

The introduction contains historical sketches of the four meetings. **(Note: There were over 200 meetings in the Philadelphia Yearly Meeting that are *not* in this volume.)** Records for Hicksite, Orthodox and Primitive Friends in these four meetings are included.

New Jersey

- Burlington MM, NJ
- Salem MM, NJ

Pennsylvania

- Falls MM, PA
- Philadelphia MM, PA

Abbreviations created specifically for Vol. II

bCLH	buried Central Laurel Hill	bSWG	buried South Western Ground
bF	buried Fallsington	bWC	buried Woodland Cemetery
bFH	buried Fair Hill	bWG	buried Western Ground
bMR	buried Marshall Road	bWLH	buried West Laurel Hill
bNLH	buried North Laurel Hill	NDMM	Philadelphia MM for the Northern District
bS	buried Salem	SDMM	Philadelphia MM for the Southern District
bSLH	buried South Laurel Hill	WDMM	Philadelphia MM for the Western District

Volume III

Volume III was published in 1940. It contains abridgments of the records for all of the meetings in New York City and on Long Island, dating from the first arrival of Friends at New Amsterdam in 1657. The records are from both the Hicksite and Orthodox branches.

New York City and Long Island

- Flushing MM, LI
- Jericho MM, LI
- New York (originally Flushing) MM, NY
- Westbury MM, LI

Abbreviations created specifically for Vol. III:

Ama.	Amawalk		Marl.	Marlboro
Balt.	Baltimore		M.C.	Musketa Cove
Beth.	Bethpage		Mk.	Matinecock
bHS	buried Houston Street		N.B.	New Bedford
Bkn.	Brooklyn		NDMM	Philadelphia MM for the Northern District
bPP	buried Prospect Park		N.E.	New England
Burl.	Burlington		N. Hemp.	North Hempstead
Chap.	Chappaqua		N.P.	Nine Partners
Cincin.	Cincinnati		O.B.	Oyster Bay
Coeym.	Coeymans		Plains.	Plainsfield
Corn.	Cornwall		Po'keepsie	Poughkeepsie
Duanesby-Duanes.	Duanesbury		Pur.	Purchase
Farm.	Farmington		Queensby.	Queensbury
Flush.	Flushing		R.&P.	Rahway & Plainfield
G.C.	Glen Cove		Renss.	Rensselaer
H.&R.	Hardwick & Randolph		Roch.	Rochester
Ham.	Hamburgh		Sara.	Saratoga
Hemp.	Hempstead		Scip.	Scipio
Hudson & Chat.	Hudson & Chatham		SDMM	Philadelphia MM for the Southern District
Jer.	Jericho		Shrews.	Shrewsbury
L.I.	Long Island		S.I.	Staten Island
Man.	Manhasset		W. & Jericho	Westbury & Jericho
			Wby	Westbury
			WDMM	Philadelphia MM for the Western District

Volume IV

Volumes IV and *V* were published simultaneously in 1946. *Volume IV* contains abstracts for half of the records for meetings in Ohio, plus a few meetings in Pennsylvania and one meeting in Michigan. All branches are included: Hicksite, Orthodox, Wilburite, and Gurneyite Friends.

Michigan
- Adriana MM, MI

Ohio
- Alum Creek MM, Delaware Co., OH
- Carmel MM, Columbiana Co., OH
- Chesterfield MM, Athens Co., OH
- Cleveland MM, Cuyahoga Co., OH
- Columbus MM, Franklin Co., OH
- Concord MM, Belmont Co., OH
- Deerfield (Pennsville) MM, Morgan Co., OH
- East Goshen MM, Mahoning Co., OH
- Flushing MM, Belmont Co., OH
- Gilead MM, Morrow Co., OH
- Goshen (Darby Creek) MM, Logan Co., OH
- Greenwich MM, Morrow Co., OH
- Marlborough MM, Stark Co., OH
- Middleton MM, Columbiana Co., OH
- New Garden MM, Columbiana Co., OH
- Plainfield MM, Belmont Co., OH
- Plymouth MM, Washington Co., OH
- Plymouth-Smithfield MM, Jefferson Co., OH
- Salem MM, Columbiana Co., OH
- Sandy Spring MM, Columbiana Co., OH
- Short Creek (Mt. Pleasant) MM, Jefferson Co., OH
- Somerset MM, Belmont Co., OH
- Stillwater MM, Belmont Co., OH
- Upper Springfield MM, Columbiana Co., OH
- West MM, Mahoning Co., OH

Pennsylvania
- Providence MM, Fayette Co., PA
- Redstone MM Fayette Co., PA
- Sewickley MM, Westmoreland Co., PA
- Westland MM, Washington Co., PA

Volume V

Volume V contains abstracts for the other half of the meetings in Ohio. Hinshaw estimated that there were more than 1 million individuals listed in the Ohio records. All branches are included: Hicksite, Orthodox, Wilburite, and Gurneyite Friends.

Ohio

- Caesar's Creek MM, Clinton Co., OH
- Center MM, Clinton Co., OH
- Cincinnati MM, Hamilton Co., OH
- Clear Creek MM, Clinton Co., OH
- Dover MM, Clinton Co., OH
- Elk MM, Preble Co., OH
- Fairfield MM, Highland Co., OH
- Fall Creek MM, Highland Co., OH
- Green Plain MM, Clark Co., OH
- Hopewell MM, Clinton Co., OH
- Lees Creek MM, Highland Co., OH
- Miami MM, Warren Co., OH
- Mill Creek MM, Miami Co., OH
- Newberry MM, Clinton Co., OH
- Springfield MM, Clinton Co., OH
- Springsborough MM, Warren Co., OH
- Union MM, Miami Co., OH
- Van Wert MM, Van Wert Co., OH
- West Branch MM, Miami Co., OH
- Westfield MM, Preble Co., OH

Volume VI

Volume VI was published in 1950, after Hinshaw's death in 1947. This volume contains abstracts for the meetings in Virginia. It is vital to note that Hinshaw had ancestors in Bedford and Campbell counties of Virginia and so decided to include abstracts of *civil marriage records* for those two counties in the back of his book of Virginia Quaker abstracts. Many people assume these are Quaker records, but they are not, so take care when using this volume as *it contains the names of hundreds of non-Quakers.* You may also want to take note that the Virginia Yearly Meeting was eventually disbanded, and the monthly meetings attached to it were then attached to the Baltimore Yearly Meeting. Those researchers interested in the early Quakers in Virginia will enjoy the history of the Virginia meetings, which is included on pages 9-15 of this volume.

Virginia

- Virginia Yearly Meeting
- Bedford Co., VA (includes marriage bonds and civil registrations of non-Quakers)
- Campbell Co., VA (includes marriage bonds and civil registration of non-Quakers)
- Alexandria MM, VA
- Black Water MM, VA (called Surry, Burley, and Gravelly Run prior to 1800)
- Camp Creek MM, VA
- Cedar Creek MM, VA (also called Caroline and Circular; now Richmond)
- Chuckatuck MM, VA (also called Nansemond)
- Crooked Run MM, VA
- Fairfax MM, VA
- Goose Creek MM (Bedford Co.), VA

- Goose Creek MM (Loudon Co.), VA
- Henrico MM, VA (also called Curles, New Kent, Upper, Upland, White Oak Swamp, and Weyanoke)
- Hopewell MM, VA (sometimes called Opeckan in early records)
- Pagan Creek MM, VA (also called Nanse-mond and Levy Neck)
- South River MM, VA (infrequently called Bedford)
- Upper MM, VA (also called Gravelly Run and Burleigh)
- Western Branch MM, VA (also called Lower and, infrequently, Buskin's)

Abbreviations created specifically for Vol. VI:

BWMM	Black Water Monthly Meeting
BWPM	Black Water Preparative Meeting
NDMM	Philadelphia MM for the Northern District
SCV	Southampton County, Virginia
SDMM	Philadelphia MM for the Western District
WDMM	Philadelphia MM for the Southern District

References and Suggested Reading

1. *Biographical Sketch of William Wade Hinshaw*, compiled for Selby Publishing & Printing Co., Kokomo, IN, 1990
2. Dixon, Ruth Priest, M.A. CGRS, "The Origins of Hinshaw's *Encyclopedia of Quaker Genealogy*," *The Pennsylvania Genealogical Magazine*, Vol. XXXIX – Number 1, Spring.Summer 1995 p. 58-64

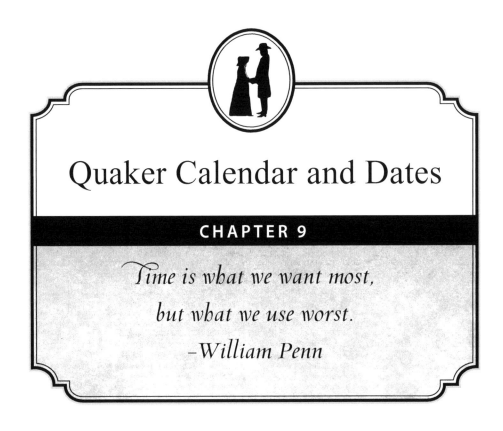

Quaker Calendar and Dates

CHAPTER 9

Time is what we want most,
but what we use worst.
–William Penn

WHEN YOU BEGIN RESEARCHING QUAKER records, you may find, as others have, that the way Quakers dated their letters, minutes, and other documents can be a bit confusing. You may even be tempted to "correct" the dates that you find when you import the information into your genealogy software. You would not be alone in thinking this way. This chapter examines the reasoning behind the Quaker calendar and dating practices of 300 years ago.

Early Friends in England objected to the names of the days and months in the English language because they considered the names to be of heathen origin. Sunday was called as such by the Saxons because it was the day they sacrificed to the sun. Monday was the day they sacrificed to the moon; Thursday was the day they sacrificed to the god Thor; and so on. Quakers thought it inconsistent for Christians to continue using the names of heathen idols. In an effort to distance themselves from these references, they created their own calendar terms using numbers, which seemed to them to be the most rational approach. Days of the week were known as "First

Day" for Sunday, "Second Day" for Monday, and so forth. Quakers attended "First Day" school, not Sunday school. They used no other names but these, either in their spoken conversations or in their letters. Similarly, the months of the year were known as "First Month" for January, "Second Month" for February, and so forth.

Upon arrival, American Friends continued this practice. As with their other efforts to reform some of society's practices that did not follow the teachings of Christ in the New Testament, Quakers did not expect people outside of the membership to conform to their ideas of how to live a Christian life. That isn't to say that they didn't share their ideas with missionary zeal and passion, but it was considered everyman's personal decision as to how he conducted his life. However, if you were a professed Quaker, you were expected to adopt these practices in your daily life.

The Julian Calendar and the Gregorian Calendar

Civilizations throughout the world were expected to change from the Julian to the Gregorian calendar in 1582, as ordered by Pope Gregory XIII. England, a predominantly Protestant country, continued using the Julian calendar and was one of the last countries to adopt the new calendar. (Germany and the Netherlands agreed to adopt the Gregorian calendar in 1698; Russia accepted it after the revolution of 1918; and Greece adopted its use in 1923.) The Julian calendar was created by (and named for) Julius Caesar in 45 B.C. and was in continuous use since that time. In the locations where it was still in use, the year officially began on March 25 and ended the following March 24.

Implementation of the *British Calendar Act of 1751* forced the calendar change in 1752. This legislation specified that starting with the year 1752, the English year would begin January 1. Thus the year 1751 began March 25, 1751, and ended December 31, 1751, which was immediately followed by January 1, 1752. To confuse things even more, there was a 12-day gap between the two calendars, so part of the *British Calendar Act of 1751* required the omission of 12 days in September of 1752, so September 2 was followed immediately by September 14.

By 1752, the Quakers in England and in the British Colonies followed this change from the Julian to the Gregorian calendar.

The problem for the modern reader is remembering that the year did not begin January 1 until 1752, meaning that until 1752, February was the "Twelfth Month" and March was the "First Month" for Quakers. As previously stated, the months September to December

Here is a helpful hint: To determine whether the record set was dated using the old (Julian) or new (Gregorian) calendar, scroll through the record set until you find a "2nd mo." entry. See if any entries were made on the 29th or 30th days of that month. If they were, then you know that the old (Julian) calendar was being used and the month would be April instead of February. You can use other months for this test as well; if you see a "7th mo." and there are entries for the 31st day, then you know that the new (Gregorian) calendar was used and the month was July, not September.

were "Seventh Month" to "Tenth Month," so those names could truthfully be used. But in 1752, when the year began in January, the old naming convention no longer applied. Therefore, from 1752, Quakers referred to *all* months by their numbers. September became "Ninth Month," December became "Twelfth Month," and so on.

Hints for Using Quaker Dating

When making notes from Quaker manuscripts, printed works, and registers, it is often helpful to write down the old-style numbers as they appear in the original text but add the new-style names afterward in square brackets for your own reference.

For example, if you see "**29 2 mo. 1731**," write it this way: "**29 2 mo. [April] 1731**."

Or if you see "**12 10 mo. 1740**," write it this way: "**12 10 mo. [December] 1740**."

Adding One More Level of Complexity
Double Dating Before 1752

Quakers in England and in the Colonies who were aware of the fact that other countries had already adopted the new calendar, often "double dated" documents by giving both their own and the Gregorian calendar year to avoid confusion.

For example, the entry "**7 11 mo. 1742**" may appear as "**7 11 mo. 1742/3**."

When making notes, you will find it useful to indicate this information in square brackets, if you are sure of which calendar the writer was using - Julian or Gregorian.

For example, the entry "**7 11 mo. 1742/3**" would be transcribed as "**7 11 mo. 1742 [January 1742/3]**" or "**7 11 mo. 1742 [November 1742/3]**"

In Summary

The best policy when researching original records is to write the dates the way that you see them. Some Quaker researchers have transposed the dates into what they thought were the "correct" dates. As you can imagine, these types of erroneous conversions could seriously affect the family stories. Misdating may lead you to assume, for example, that a woman was pregnant prior to marriage or that the children were born after the family moved to a new meeting when, in fact, neither was true.

	Rest of the World Wrote	Quaker Terms Were Written	Rest of the World Wrote	Quaker Terms Were Written
	Julian (pre-1752)	Julian (pre-1752)	Gregorian (post-1752)	Gregorian (post-1752)
March (first day of the year was March 25)	1st month, March	i or 1 mo.	3rd month, March	iii or 3rd mo.
April	2nd month, April	ii or 2 mo.	4th month, April	iv or 4th mo.
May	3rd month, May	iii or 3 mo.	5th month, May	v or 5th mo.
June	4th month, June	iv or 4 mo.	6th month, June	vi or6th mo.
July	5th month, July	v or 5 mo.	7th month, July	vii or 7th mo.
August	6th month, August	vi or 6 mo.	8th month, August	viii or 8th mo.
September	7th month, September	vii or 7 mo.	9th month, September	ix or 9th mo.
October	8th month, October	viii or 8 mo.	10th month, October	x or 10th mo.
November	9th month, November	ix or 9 mo.	11th month, November	xi or 11th mo.
December	10th month, December	x or 10 mo.	12th month, December	xii or 12th mo.
January	11th month, January	xi or 11 mo.	1st month, January	i or 1st mo.
February	12th month, February	xii or 12 mo.	2nd month, February	ii or 2nd mo.

FIGURE 9-1: Use this chart to help determine the correct month when researching early Quaker records.

Quakers	1st Day	2nd Day	3rd Day	4th Day	5th Day	6th Day	7th Day
Non-Quakers	Sunday	Monday	Tuesday	Wednesday	Thursday	Friday	Saturday

FIGURE 9-2: Conversion Chart to Determine Correct Day when researching early Quaker records.

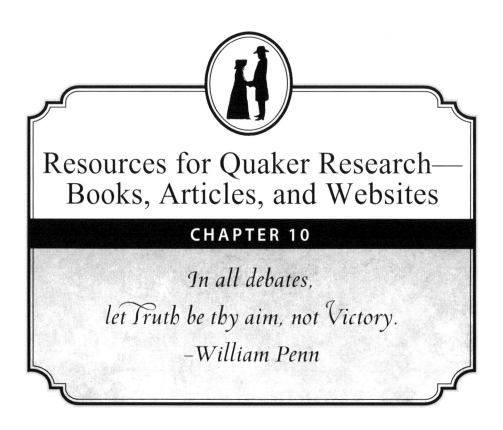

Resources for Quaker Research—Books, Articles, and Websites

CHAPTER 10

*In all debates,
let Truth be thy aim, not Victory.*
–William Penn

THIS CHAPTER FOCUSES ON RESOURCES that are currently available to Quaker researchers. It includes online resources that provide excellent tools and physical repositories that offer findings aids (books and articles) about Quaker meetings.

Researchers who have found an ancestor in the Quaker records may be interested in learning more about the ancestor and the meeting he or she attended. Many excellent finding aids have been written about specific meetings. The list that follows is by no means exhaustive, but it highlights some of the resources available for those individuals who are doing more in-depth research. You would benefit from making use of the books that are written about records in your area of interest, by authors who have worked with these records for years and can tell you a lot about them.

For instance, if you are researching Quakers in Delaware, look for Herbert Standing's excellent book *Delaware Quaker Records: Early Members of Northern New Castle County.* (See the finding aids under "Delaware.") Perhaps you are researching in Georgia; look for the reference to William Medlin's book about the Quakers in Georgia and South Carolina. (See the finding aids under "Georgia.") If you are researching New York Quakers, be sure to look under "Online Resources" for a reference to the "Hazard Index," which is an index of *every name* that is found listed in the New York Yearly Meeting records. What a great gift this resource is to New York researchers!

With so many Quaker meeting records digitized and online, it is an amazing time to be researching Quaker genealogical records. After you find the books for the state or area you are researching, talk to your librarian about borrowing them through inter-library loan. In some cases, you may need to contact a historical society to buy a copy of a work they have printed. You can usually find the societies' contact details online.

If you are interested in viewing a copy of a published book on Quaker research such as those listed in this chapter, go to http://freepages.genealogy.rootsweb.com/~jrichmon/quaker/qksrcsec.htm. There you can see if Jerry Richmond has the book in his extensive book list, which is arranged by publisher. It's an easy way to see whether it is still in print. Jerry also has a list of manuscripts that are on microfilm at the Family History Library in Salt Lake City. You can order these microfilms to be sent to your local LDS Family History Center for viewing.

Online Sources

Hazard Index to New York Yearly Meeting records

This is an excellent, fairly recent resource created for those searching for Quaker ancestors from the New York state area. James E. Hazard, working with the original records at Friends Historical Library of Swarthmore College, extracted all pertinent details from the records of the New York Yearly Meeting. The "Hazard Index" includes all of the early monthly meeting minutes. It is available at Swarthmore.edu. The full web address is: http://www.swarthmore.edu/library/friends/hazard/.

QuakerMeetings.com

This website is another recent resource to aid people researching their Quaker ancestors. Tom Hill compiled a terrific index that includes the basic information about every monthly meeting of the Religious Society of Friends that has ever existed in North America. He has captured vital information, such as: meeting name, any former meeting names, parent bodies, Hicksite or Orthodox affiliation, location address, meeting records storage locations, which meeting books are extant, and microfilm numbers (if filmed).

QuakerMeetings.com is an easy and convenient way to search for information about any monthly meeting. It is frequently updated, whenever new information is obtained.

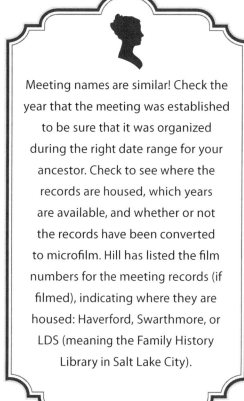

Meeting names are similar! Check the year that the meeting was established to be sure that it was organized during the right date range for your ancestor. Check to see where the records are housed, which years are available, and whether or not the records have been converted to microfilm. Hill has listed the film numbers for the meeting records (if filmed), indicating where they are housed: Haverford, Swarthmore, or LDS (meaning the Family History Library in Salt Lake City).

HOW TO USE:

There are four tabs at the top: Home, Meeting Search, Data Definitions, and Yearly Meetings.

The Data Definitions and Yearly Meetings tabs are good reference tools and will help you understand background details of the website and of any yearly meeting in North America.

The Meeting Search tab is what you will use to search for information about the meeting your ancestor attended. *If you do not know the name of the meeting he or she attended*: enter the state and county with no meeting name. You will see a list of all the meetings in the county and might see one named for the town where he or she lived. Click on that meeting name to learn more about it. *If you do know the name of the meeting he attended*: enter the meeting name with the appropriate county and state.

Much of the information from Quakermeetings.com can be accessed on Ancestry.com under the title: *U.S. and Canada, Quaker Monthly Meetings Index, 1671–2010.*

Meeting name	State or Province	County	Physical location
BURLINGTON (ORTHODOX)	NEW JERSEY	BURLINGTON	BURLINGTON 08016, 340 HIGH ST. NEAR BROAD
CHESTER (HICKSITE)	NEW JERSEY	BURLINGTON	MOORESTOWN 08057
CHESTERFIELD (HICKSITE)	NEW JERSEY	BURLINGTON	CROSSWICKS 08515, HANOVER STREET
CROPWELL	NEW JERSEY	BURLINGTON	MARLTON 08053, 802 S. CROPWELL RD.
CROSSWICKS	NEW JERSEY	BURLINGTON	CROSSWICKS 08015, 15 FRONT ST.
EVESHAM (HICKSITE)	NEW JERSEY	BURLINGTON	MOUNT LAUREL 08054
EVESHAM (ORTHODOX)	NEW JERSEY	BURLINGTON	MOUNT LAUREL 08054, MOORESTOWN-MT. LAUREL RD.
MEDFORD	NEW JERSEY	BURLINGTON	MEDFORD 08055, 14 UNION ST.
MOORESTOWN	NEW JERSEY	BURLINGTON	MOORESTOWN 08057, 118 MAIN ST.
MOUNT HOLLY (HICKSITE)	NEW JERSEY	BURLINGTON	MOUNT HOLLY 08060, HIGH & GARDEN STS.
MOUNT HOLLY (ORTHODOX)	NEW JERSEY	BURLINGTON	MOUNT HOLLY 08060
RANCOCAS	NEW JERSEY	BURLINGTON	RANCOCAS 08073, 201 MAIN ST.
UPPER EVESHAM (ORTHODOX)	NEW JERSEY	BURLINGTON	MEDFORD 08055
UPPER SPRINGFIELD (HICKSITE)	NEW JERSEY	BURLINGTON	COLUMBUS 08022, S.R. 206
UPPER SPRINGFIELD (ORTHODOX)	NEW JERSEY	BURLINGTON	MANSFIELD 08022
WESTFIELD	NEW JERSEY	BURLINGTON	CINNAMINSON 08077, 2201 RIVERTON RD. & US 130

FIGURE 10-1: All meetings in Burlington County, New Jersey. If the name of the meeting your ancestor attended is not known, search a list of all meetings in their county and see which one was the closest geographically. Image from QuakerMeetings.com.

Quaker Group Lists on Rootsweb.com

Rootsweb.com, which is a free site hosted by Ancestry.com, is an excellent resource for Quaker research. Rootsweb.com has hundreds of message boards and group mailing lists that you can join for free with just your email address. Two mailing lists that are particularly helpful to Quaker researchers are Quaker Roots and PA-Quakers. After you register, which is a very simple process, you will begin receiving emails from other group members who are asking questions or giving answers to questions from others. You don't ever have to post a question or answer one, but you can learn from reading the conversations of others. In fact, the archives of the mailing list Quaker Roots contain hundreds of subjects discussed by less-experienced researchers asking questions of the members of the group.

For example, this is the kind of help available through these online groups:

One gentleman was planning to travel across the country to visit the Quaker burying ground of his ancestors in Pennsylvania. He posted a question to the group asking where to find the records of the cemetery and perhaps a plat map. He received many responses from experienced researchers and from people who had lived in the area. They pointed him in the right direction by giving information on where to find the records of that meeting, whom to contact, and the

QuakerMeetings.com

"Monthly Meetings in North America: A Quaker Index"

Home | Meeting Search | Data Definitions | Yearly Meetings

You are here: Home

Meeting name: ABINGTON (HICKSITE)
Website: http://www.pym.org/abington-qm/abingtonmm.htm
Records Website: http://trilogy.brynmawr.edu/speccoll/mm/abingmm.xml
Preparative Records: http://trilogy.brynmawr.edu/speccoll/mm/abingpm.xml
Former meeting names
TACKONY & POETQUESINK UNTIL 1685
OXFORD OR CHELTENHAM 1683 - 1687
DUBLIN 1687 - 1710/06/24

State or Province: PENNSYLVANIA
County: MONTGOMERY
Physical location: JENKINTOWN 19046, 520 MEETINGHOUSE RD.
Latitude: 40.09281 N **Longitude:** 075.11795 W

Date granted: 1683/06/05
Date of first meeting: 1683/09/03
Current Status: ACTIVE
Before and After: ABINGTON (CHELTENHAM) WORSHIP 1683/12. PM 1702/02-1943.

Branches
[HICKSITE] 1827/09/24 - 1827/09/24

Latest yearly meeting: PHILADELPHIA Y.M.
Where records are kept: SWARTHMORE mf HAVERFORD. LDS 20375, 20453, 21673, 383428-30.
Records known extant: SWARTHMORE: MIN 1682-1782, 1797-1975, WOMEN MIN 1773-1893, BIRTHS 1670-1812, BIRTHS & DEATHS 1780-19
1764-1837, M&E 1713-1827
Affiliations
PHILADELPHIA Q.M. UNTIL 1786/02/06
ABINGTON Q.M. AFTER 1786/05/04
Local-related histories:
Comments: BOUND JAMES E. HAZARD COMPLETE-NAME GENEALOGICAL ABSTRACTS AT FRIENDS HISTORICAL LIBRARY, SWARTHMORE, PA.
Subordinates
BYBERRY PM 1701-1782.
FRANKFORD (OXFORD, TACKONY) PM 1701/11-1816.
GERMANTOWN PM 1728-1816.
HORSHAM PM 1717-1782.

FIGURE 10-2: Check QuakerMeetings.com for a list of former names of the meeting, and to see which records still exist and where they are.

condition of the cemetery and its records. This man's experience is a fairly common occurrence on the Quaker Roots group list. There is no cost involved to join, and you will likely meet helpful people who are searching for their ancestors, just like you.

You may find it helpful to explore these excellent websites, as well:

Quaker Electronic Archive (http://www.qis.net/~daruma/)
Quaker Corner (http://www.rootsweb.ancestry.com/~quakers/)

Cyndi's List (http://www.CyndisList.com/quaker.htm)
Religious Society of Friends (http://www.quaker.org)

Quaker Records in Canada and the United Kingdom

CANADA

All filmed meeting records from Pickering College will be part of the Quaker Collection on Ancestry.com.

Repository:	**Quaker Archives and Library of Canada**
Location:	Pickering College, 16945 Bayview Avenue, Newmarket, Ontario, L3Y 4X2, Canada
Phone:	905-895-1700 x. 247
Email:	*cym-archivist@quaker.ca*
Website:	http://www.archives-library.quaker.ca/en/introduction.html

Collection Details: The Canadian Yearly Meeting Archives consist of the business and genealogical records of the yearly meeting and its associated half-yearly, quarterly, monthly, and preparative meetings, dating from the establishment of the first meeting in 1798.

Note: Before the formation of Canadian Yearly Meeting, its predecessor yearly meetings deposited most of their U.S. meeting records in the New York Yearly Meeting Archives, which was moved in 1997 to Swarthmore.

Finding Aids:

- Briggs, Elizabeth, *Access to Ancestry: A Genealogical Resource Manual for Canadians Tracing their Heritage.* Winnipeg: Westgarth, 1995
- Dorland, Arthur G., *A History of the Society of Friends (Quakers) in Canada* (1927) and *The Quakers in Canada: A History,* Toronto (1968)
- MacMaster, Richard, *Friends in the Niagara Peninsula, 1786-1802, a very interesting article on the Canada website listed above, regarding the migration and settling of Canadian Quakers.*
- Mekeel, Arthur. "Quaker-Loyalist Migration to New Brunswick and Nova Scotia in 1783." *Bulletin of Friends Historical Association,* v. 32, p. 65-75 and v. 37, p. 26-38.

ENGLAND

All registers from The National Archives at Pew are in the Quaker Collection on Ancestry.com.

Repository:	**Friends House, London**
Location:	173 - 177 Euston Road, London, NW1 2BJ, England
Phone:	+44 (0)020 7663 1135
Email:	library@quaker.org.uk
Website:	http://www.quaker.org.uk
Collection Details:	The library houses archived meeting records for the London and Middlesex Yearly Meetings, including copies of the digests of the earliest Quaker records.

Ancestry.com has the Quaker records from original registers (1600 in total) that have been archived at The National Archives at Kew. **Title on Ancestry.com:** *England & Wales, Quaker Birth, Marriage, and Death Registers, 1578-1837.* They are from Record Group 6, Records of the General Register Office.

Important points to remember when using this collection: The registers are not a complete record of all Quaker records in England and Wales for this period. Several dozen extant registers were not surrendered and many registers were lost. There may be gaps in the registers, especially during the period of 1710 to 1775, and particularly for marriages. It is wise to check the minute books of a particular meeting for that time period, which are maintained either by the meeting or have been deposited with the local County Record Office.

Repository:	**The Quaker Library at Woodbrooke**
Location:	1046 Bristol Road, Selly Oak, Birmingham 29 6LJ, England
Phone:	44-0-121-472-5171
Email:	enquiries@woodbrooke.org.uk
Website:	http://www.woodbrooke.org.uk
Collection Details:	Second only to Friends House Library in the wealth of its holdings, this library consists of about 10,000 items dating from the 17th century to the present day. Together with the Bevan-Naish Collection, it contains over half of all items published in the 17th century by Quakers. The Bevan-Naish Collection consists of early books, tracts, and a few manuscripts by Quaker authors and on Quaker topics, many of them 17th and 18th century.

Repository:	**Society of Genealogists**
Location:	14 Charterhouse Buildings, Goswell Road, London EC1M 7BA, UK
Phone:	44-20-7251-8799
Email:	genealogy@sog.org.uk
Website:	http://www.sog.org.uk/index.shtml
Collection Details:	This library is the foremost in the British Isles, with a large collection of

family histories, civil registration and census material, and the widest collection of county sources in the country (over 9000).

IRELAND

Repository:	**Historical Library at Quaker House**
Location:	Stocking Lane, Rathfarnham, Dublin 16
Phone:	353-01-495-6890
Email:	qhist@eircom.net
Website:	http://www.quakers-in-ireland.ie/index.htm
Collection Details:	The Friends' Historical Library is the repository for the manuscript

records of Quakers in Ireland. It has registers of births, marriages, and burials from the 1600s to the present. The manuscripts include title deeds and minute books of meetings throughout Ireland, together with letters, wills, pedigrees, photographs, and other personal material.

Enquiries regarding Quaker archives and records for Ulster should be addressed to: Ulster Quarterly Meeting Archives Committee, 4 Magheralave Road, Lisburn, Ireland, BT28 3BD.

Finding Aids:

- Myers, Albert Cook, *Immigration of the Irish Quakers into Pennsylvania 1682 - 1750,* Swarthmore, PA, 1902. A must-read for those interested in the early Quakers in Ireland, ***this book is available on Ancestry.com***, where it can be read and searched by name. Myers has included a list of almost 25,000 names of those Quakers who emigrated from Ireland. It has numerous biographical sketches of prominent Irish Quakers and abstracts of Certificates of Removal from various monthly meetings in Ireland and where they settled in Pennsylvania.

- Goodbody, Olive C., *Guide to Irish Quaker Records, 1654-1860: With Contribution on Northern Ireland Records by B. G. Hutton,* Clearfield Co, July 1999. This amazing resource contains a list of all 2250 surnames appearing in Irish Quaker meeting registers and a complete name index of more than 5000 names.

SCOTLAND

Repository: **New Register House**

Location: 3 West Register Street, Edinburgh , Scotland , EH1 3YT

Contact Form: http://www.gro-scotland.gov.uk/contacts/contact-form.html

Website: http://www.scan.org.uk/

Background: There were two yearly meetings in Scotland, one in Aberdeen and one in Edinburgh. In 1786, they became part of the London Yearly Meeting and were combined into the North Britain Half Years Meeting. In 1807, it was given the name of the Scotland General Meeting. Quaker meetings in Scotland did not have to surrender their meeting records to the government. In 1867, a digest was finally created and submitted to the Record Office. The original records are still with the meeting.

Finding Aids:

- Dobson, David, *Scottish Quakers and Early America, 1650-1700*, GPC, 1998 **(available on Ancestry.com)**. This book identifies members of the Society of Friends in Scotland prior to 1700 and the Scottish origins of many of the Quakers who settled in East Jersey in the 1680s.
- For a list of Scottish settlers who came to the Colonies and Canada, **check on Ancestry.com** in the *Directory of Scottish Settlers in North America, 1625-1825*. Vols. I-VII.

UNITED STATES *(alphabetized by state)*

CALIFORNIA

Repository: Whittier College, Wardman Library, Quaker Collection

Location: Whittier, CA 90608

Phone: (562) 907-4247

Website: http://www.whittier.edu/library/

Collection Details: Whittier College was founded by members of the Religious Society of Friends in the late 19th century. The Quaker Collection originated with contributions from these early founders and has grown to become the largest historical archive of Quaker materials in the western United States. With holdings of over 6000 books and periodicals, it is also the largest of the college's Special Collections. The core of the collection consists of an extensive set of personal narratives and diaries, Quaker regional histories, family genealogies, meeting minutes, periodicals, and reference materials. A description of the general reference sources as well as regional publications used in conducting genealogical research can be found in the guide, "Genealogical Sources in the Quaker Collection, Whittier College."

Finding Aids:

- *Quakers in California* by David C. LeShana (1969). Covers the background and founding of the yearly meeting, with references to monthly meetings and their establishment.

DELAWARE
All available meeting records are in the Quaker Collection on Ancestry.com.

Finding Aids:

- *Friends in Wilmington, 1738-1938*, Wilmington, DE: Charles L. Story Company, 1938. This book gives a history of the meeting and lists many of the early individuals interred in the burial ground.
- Standing, Herbert, comp. *Delaware Quaker Records: Early Members of Northern New Castle County*,1970

GEORGIA
All available meeting records are in the Quaker Collection on Ancestry.com.

Finding Aids:

- Hitz, Alex M. "The Wrightsborough Quaker Town and Township in Georgia." *Bulletin of Friends Historical Association,* v. 46, p. 10-22
- Medlin, William F. *Quaker Families of South Carolina and Georgia*. South Carolina, Ben Franklin Press, c1982

ILLINOIS

Finding Aids:

- *Quaker records: Illinois monthly meetings,* 1900. Records of Chicago area meetings, only. **This book is searchable by name on Ancestry.com.**

INDIANA

All available meeting records are in the Quaker Collection on Ancestry.com.

Finding Aids:

- Boone, Roger S. *Additions, Corrections & Comments: Abstracts of the Records of the Society of Friends in Indiana, Parts 1 - 6,* Springfield, OH, 1978
- Dorrel, Ruth & Thomas D. Hamm, ed. *Abstracts of the Records of the Society of*
- *Friends in Indiana,* vol. 1, Indiana Historical Society, Indianapolis, IN, 1996
- Heiss, Willard C. *A List of All the Friends Meetings That Exist or Ever Have Existed in Indiana* 1807-1955, Indianapolis, IN, 1961
- Heiss, Willard C. *Guide to Research in Quaker Records in the Midwest,* Willard Heiss, Indiana History Bulletin, March/April, 1962
- Heiss, Willard C., comp. *Abstracts of Records of the Society of Friends in Indiana*, Vol. VII of *Encyclopedia of American Quaker Genealogy* (7 vols.), Indianapolis: Indiana Historical Society, 1977. These volumes cover the meetings in Indiana and eastern Illinois. This volume is based on the original records, not Hinshaw's, although the abstracts are identical in format to those of Hinshaw.
- Lindley, Harlow. "A Century of Indiana Yearly Meeting." *Bulletin of Friends' Historical Association,* v. 12, p. 3-21
- Ratcliff, Richard P. *Our Special Heritage: Sesquicentennial History of Friends (Quakers).* New Castle, IN, 1970
- Samuelson, W. David. *Society of Friends (Quaker) Records of Fairfield Monthly Meeting, 1786-1879, Hendricks and Marion Counties, Indiana.* Salt Lake City: Kokaubeam Co., 1988

IOWA

Repository: Wilcox Library, William Penn College
Location: 201 Trueblood Ave, Oskaloosa, IA 52577

Phone: 800-779-7366
Website: http://www.wmpenn.edu/Library/library.html
Collection Details: This resource is the Quaker Collection at the Wilcox Library of William Penn College. Monthly meeting records for the Iowa Yearly Meeting are held at the Yearly Meeting Office, although they are not complete because some local meetings have retained their records.

Finding Aids:

- *Spiritual Trails of a People Called Friends: Book II* (1988), a 125th anniversary booklet that contains a chart and a map of monthly meetings.
- Cook, Darius B. *Memoirs of Quaker Divide.* Dexter, Iowa: The Dexter Sentinel, 1914
- Jones, Louis Thomas. *The Quakers of Iowa*. 1914. Reprint, Bowie, Maryland: Heritage Books, 1999

KANSAS

Repository: **The Edmund Stanley Library, Friends University**
Location: 2100 W. University St., Wichita, KS 67213
Phone: 1-800-794-6945
Collection Details: The Quaker Room, Edmund Stanley Library, Friends University, Wichita, Kansas is the repository for the archives of the Mid-American Yearly Meeting. Kansas Yearly Meeting opened 1872, set off from Indiana (Orthodox) Yearly Meeting. It changed its name to Mid-America Yearly Meeting in 1978.

MAINE

Maine Historical Society Library

Collection Details: Many of the records of Maine meetings have been deposited here. The earlier records have, for the most part, been filmed and are available at both the Rhode Island and Maine Historical Society libraries.

Finding Aids:

- Jones, Rufus Matthew, *The Society of Friends in Kennebec County, Maine.* New York: H.W. Blake & Co., 1992. **This book is on Ancestry.com.**

MARYLAND

All available meeting records are in the Quaker Collection on Ancestry.com.

Finding Aids:

- Beard, Alice L., comp. *Births, deaths, and marriages of the Nottingham Quakers, 1680-1889.* Westminster, Md.: Family Line Publications, 1989
- Carroll, Kenneth Lane. "Quakerism in Caroline County, Maryland: Its Rise and Decline." *Bulletin of Friends' Historical Association*, V. 48, p. 83-102
- Carroll, Kenneth Lane. *Quakerism on the Eastern Shore.* Baltimore: Maryland Historical Society, 1970
- Forbush, Bliss. *A History of Baltimore Yearly Meeting of Friends* (1972), contains the authorized history, maps, and some data on monthly meetings.
- Jacobsen, Phebe R. *Quaker Records in Maryland.* Annapolis: The Hall of Records Commission, 1966. This book lists all the microfilmed records and their reel numbers at the Hall of Records in Annapolis and provides historical sketches of meetings.
- McGhee, Lucy Kate. *Maryland Quaker (Friends): records of Third Haven (Tred Avon) Talbot County.* Washington, D.C., 1950. **This book is on Ancestry.com.**

MASSACHUSETTS (See also: New England)

Finding Aids:

- Dillingham, John H. *The Society of Friends in Barnstable County, Massachusetts.* New York: H.W. Blake & Co., 1891. **This book is on Ancestry.com.**
- Hallowell, Richard P. *Quaker Invasion of Massachusetts.* Boston, MA, USA: Houghton, Mifflin and Company, 1883. **This book is on Ancestry.com.**
- Pestana, Carla Gardina. *Quakers and Baptists in Colonial Massachusetts,* Cambridge Press, 1991

MICHIGAN

Many meeting records for this state are in the Quaker Collection on Ancestry.com.

Finding Aids:

- Burton, Ann, and Conrad Burton, comp. *Michigan Quakers: Abstracts of Fifteen Meetings of the Society of Friends, 1831-1960*. Decatur, MI: Glyndwr [sic] Resources, 1989

NEW ENGLAND

Repository: **Rhode Island Historical Society Library,**

Location: Providence, Rhode Island

Website: http://www.rihs.org

Collection Details: The Archives of the New England Yearly Meeting of the Society of Friends are housed at the Rhode Island Historical Society Library. The records cover most of the Quaker meetings in New England from 1676 to the present, including vital records and meeting minutes.

Finding Aids:

- Hallowell, Richard P. *The Quaker Invasion of Massachusetts*. c1883. Reprint, Bowie, MD: Heritage Books, 1987
- Hinchman, Lydia Swain Mitchell, comp. *Early Settlers of Nantucket, Their Associates and Descendants*. 1934. Reprint, Rutland VT: C. E. Tuttle Co., 1980
- Stattler, Richard D. *Guide to the Records of Religious Society of Friends (Quakers) in New England* (1997). Stattler's book contains a sketch of meeting histories and maps and is for sale at the Rhode Island Historical Society.
- Weeks, Silas. *New England Quaker Meetinghouses*. Richmond, Indiana, 2001
- Worrall, Arthur J. *Quakers in the Colonial Northeast*. Hanover, N.H.: University Press of New England, 1980

NEW JERSEY

All filmed meeting records are in the Quaker Collection on Ancestry.com.

Finding Aids:

- Gross, Diana, ed., *Woodstown Friends Meeting*, 1785-1985. (1985)
- Gummere, Amelie Mott, *Friends in Burlington* (1884)
- Irwin, Richard T. *A history: the Religious Society of Friends in Randolph Township*. New Jersey, 1983. **This book is on Ancestry.com.**
- Meldrum, Charlotte. *Early Church Records of Burlington County, New Jersey*, 3 vols. Family

Line Publications, 1995. Includes most of the early Friends' meetings in the colony of West Jersey.

NEW YORK

Many meeting records for this state are in book form in the Quaker Collection on Ancestry. com.

Collection Details: The Haviland Records Room was the official archives for the New York Yearly Meeting. Its holdings were moved to the Friends Historical Library at Swarthmore College in 1997.

Finding Aids:

- Barbour, Hugh. *Quaker Crosscurrents: Three Hundred Years of Friends in the New York Yearly Meetings* by Hugh Barbour. (Syracuse University Press, 1995) This book includes maps and lists of meetings as of 1828.
- Bradley, A. Day. "New York Yearly Meeting at Poplar Ridge and the Primitive Friends." *Quaker History* 68, 2 (1979)
- Cox, John Jr. *A catalog of the records in possession of, or relating to, the two New York Yearly Meetings of the Religious Society of Friends and their subordinate meetings.* New York: Historical Records Survey, WPA, 1940. Includes information on monthly meetings and records prior to the 1930s.
- Cox, John, Jr. "Quaker Records in New York," *The New York Genealogical and Biographical Record.* V. 45, 1914, p. 263-269, 366-373
- Eardeley, William Applebie. *Amawalk, Westchester County, New York, Friends Monthly Meeting records: births, marriages and deaths, 1724-1908.* Brooklyn, N.Y.1914. **This book is on Ancestry.com.**
- Fay, Loren. *Quaker census of 1828: members of the New York Yearly Meeting, the Religious Society of Friends in New York, Ontario, Vermont, Connecticut, Massachusetts, and Quebec, at the time of the separation of 1828.* You will find an extensive and comprehensive list of all members of the New York Yearly Meeting in alphabetical order, with their monthly meetings.
- Frost, Josephine. *Quaker marriages, Jericho Monthly Meeting, Long Island, New York*, 1991. **This book is on Ancestry.com.**

- Hazard, James E. http://www.swarthmore.edu/Library/friends/hazard, an every-name index to all of the monthly meeting minutes in the New York Yearly Meeting records.
- Moger, Elizabeth H. "Records of New York Yearly Meeting of the Society of Friends and the Haviland Records Room, New York City," *Tree Talks* 25 (March 1985):3-22
- Spies, Francis F. *Chappaqua, N.Y., Quaker records.* Mount Vernon, N.Y.,: unknown, 1990. **This book is on Ancestry.com.**
- Spies, Francis F. *Inscriptions from Quaker burying grounds with notes: Purchase, West Chester Co., Chappaqua, West Chester Co., Pawling, Dutchess Co., (Quaker Hill), Bethel, Dutchess Co., index.* Mt. Vernon, N.Y., 1989. **This book is on Ancestry.com.**

NORTH CAROLINA

All filmed meeting records are in the Quaker Collection on Ancestry.com.

Repository:	**Friends Historical Collection, Hege Library**
Location:	Guilford College, 5800 W. Friendly Ave., Greensboro, NC 27410
Phone:	336-316-2264
Email:	hegefhc@guilford.edu.
Website:	http://library.guilford.edu/friends-historical-collection

Collection Details: The North Carolina Yearly Meeting included meetings in North and South Carolina, Georgia, southern Virginia, and eastern Tennessee.

Finding Aids:

- Anscombe, Francis Charles. *I Have Called You Friends: The Story of Quakerism in North Carolina.* Boston: Christopher Pub., 1959
- Bjorkman, Gwen Boyer. *Quaker Marriage Certificates Pasquotank, Perquimans, Piney Woods, and Suttons Creek s...Monthly Meetings, North Carolina, 1677-1800.* Bowie, MD: Heritage Books, 1988. These records are essential for those researching their Quaker roots as they contain not only names of brides and grooms, but also an extensive listing of witnesses and attendees, providing a partial census of friends and family of the brides and grooms.
- Gilbert, Dorothy Lloyd. *Guilford, a Quaker college,* 1937. **This book is on Ancestry.com.**
- Hilty, Hiram H. *By Land and by Sea Quakers Confront Slavery and its Aftermath in North Carolina,* North Carolina Friends Historical Society, Greensboro, NC, 1993

- Hinshaw, Seth B. *The Carolina Quaker Experience, 1665-1985.* NC Yearly Meeting and NC Friends Historical Society, 1984
- Perkins, Theodore Edison, *Marriages in Contentnea Quarterly Meeting of Friends*
- *North Carolina Yearly Meeting 1737-1891*, Guilford County Genealogical Society, Greensboro, NC, 1988
- Winslow, Raymond A. Jr. "Early Quakers, the Society of Friends in Colonial Perquimans," in *Perquimans County History.* Hertford, NC: Perquimans County Restoration Association, 1984

OHIO
All filmed meeting records are in the Quaker Collection on Ancestry.com.

Finding Aids:
- *Clarkson Butterworth List [of] 1905.* Lists in alphabetical order all meetings that ever belonged to the Indiana Yearly Meeting, omitting meetings of Orthodox Friends after the Separation of 1827. This is an extensive list with fascinating details about the founding of the many meetings in this yearly meeting. See this website: www2.wilmington.edu/academics/ThomasC.HillsAreaQuakerHistoryResources.cfm.
- Morlan, Charles P. *A Brief History of Ohio Yearly Meeting of the Religious Society of Friends (Conservative).* Barnesville, Ohio: Representative Meeting of Ohio Yearly Meeting, Religious Society of Friends, 1959
- Smith, H. E. "The Quakers, Their Migration to the Upper Ohio, Their Customs and Discipline." *Ohio State Archaeological and Historical Society Quarterly,* v, XXXCII, no. 1, Jan 1928, p. 35-85
- Snarr, D. Neil. *Claiming Our Past: Quakers in Southwest Ohio and Eastern Tennessee*
- Taber, William. *The Eye of Faith: A History of Ohio Yearly Meeting, Conservative.* Barnesville, Ohio: Representative Meeting of Ohio Yearly Meeting, Religious Society of Friends, 1985

OREGON

Repository:	**Quaker Collection, Murdoch Library, George Fox University**
Location:	414 N. Meridian Street, Newberg, OR 97132
Phone:	503-538-8383
Website:	http://www.georgefox.edu/

Collection Details: The Northwest Yearly Meeting has stored most of its records in a vault located in the Newberg Friends Church and a small collection at George Fox University's Murdoch Library. The archives of Northwest Yearly Meeting of Friends Church, dating from the 1880s, are preserved in the Church Archives Room in Sutton Hall.

Finding Aids:

* Beebe, Ralph K. *A Garden of the Lord: A History of Oregon Yearly Meeting of Friends Church* (1968). Contains histories of monthly meetings.

PENNSYLVANIA

Preparatory and monthly meeting records are included in the Quaker Collection on Ancestry.com.

There are two repositories for Quaker records in this region: Haverford College Quaker Collection (http://www.haverford.edu/library/special/collections/quaker/) and the Swarthmore Friends Historical Library, housed in the McCabe Library on the Swarthmore College campus. The Quaker Collection at Swarthmore College is the largest in the United States and includes the records of the Philadelphia, Baltimore, Virginia, and Ohio yearly meetings. Swarthmore also has microfilm of Quaker records from several yearly meetings from other locations.

Note: These records are now on Ancestry.com.

Repository:	**Swarthmore Friends Historical Library**
Location:	Swarthmore College, 500 College Avenue, Swarthmore, PA 19081
Phone:	610-328-8497
Email:	friends@swarthmore.edu
Website:	http://www.swarthmore.edu/academics/friends-historical-library.xml

Swarthmore has online finding aids for the following yearly meetings:

* Baltimore Yearly Meeting
* Genesee Yearly Meeting
* Illinois Yearly Meeting (Hicksite)
* Lake Erie Yearly Meeting
* New York Yearly Meeting
* Ohio Yearly Meeting (Hicksite)
* Pacific Yearly Meeting
* Philadelphia Yearly Meeting
* South Central Yearly Meeting
* Southern Appalachia Yearly Meeting

This link provides an excellent guide to the records of the Philadelphia Yearly Meeting: http://trilogy.brynmawr.edu/speccoll/pymmm.htm.

This is a partial list of the many excellent books and guides written about the Pennsylvania Quakers and their meetings.

Finding Aids:

- *A Collection of Memorials Concerning Divers Deceased Ministers and Others of the People Called Quakers.* Philadelphia: Joseph Crukshank, Printer, 1787. Covers areas of Pennsylvania and New Jersey from 1682 to 1787. Similar volumes are available for other areas.
- Bjorkman, Gwen Boyer. Quaker *Marriage Certificates: Concord Monthly Meeting, Delaware County, Pennsylvania, 1679-1808.* These abstracts of early marriage records name all participants, including lists of witnesses, and have a name and place index, as well as two maps showing the locations of individual meeting houses. 1991
- Bjorkman, Gwen Boyer. *Quaker Marriage Certificates: New Garden Monthly Meeting, Chester County, PA 1704-1799* (1990)
- Brown, George Williams. *Historical sketches chiefly relating to the early settlement of Friends at Falls, in Bucks County, Pennsylvania.* 1981. **This book is on Ancestry.com.**
- Browning, Charles H. *Welsh Tract of Pennsylvania: The Early Settlers....* Westminster, MD: Family Line Publications, 1990
- Bunting, Morgan. *A list of the records of the meetings constituting the yearly meeting of the Society of Friends: held at Fifteenth and Race Streets, Philadelphia.* Philadelphia: Printed for the Representative Committee, 1984. **This book is on Ancestry.com.**
- Eckert, Jack D., comp. *A Guide to the Records of Philadelphia Yearly Meeting.* Family Line Publications, 1989. Virtually a complete listing of Quaker records available for Pennsylvania and New Jersey, held at the two Quaker repositories, Swarthmore and Haverford. Glenn, Thomas Allen, *Welsh Founders of Pennsylvania,* Oxford: Fox, Jones and Co., 1911-1913. **This book is on Ancestry.com.**
- Glenn, Thomas Allen. *Merion in the Welsh Tract, with Sketches of the Townships of Haverford and Radnor. Historical and Genealogical Collections Concerning the Welsh Barony in the Province of Pennsylvania Settled by the Cymric Quakers in 1682.* Partial index, 1896 Reprint 2006, Genealogical Publishing Co.
- *Gwynedd Monthly Meeting of the Religious Society of Friends, 1699-1949: two hundred and*

*fiftieth anniversary, Gwynedd, Montgomery Co., Pennsylvania,*1949. **This book is on Ancestry.com.**

- Heiss, Willard, ed. *Quaker Biographical Sketches of Ministers and Elders, and*
- *Other Concerned Members of the Yearly Meeting of Philadelphia 1682-1800*, Indianapolis, Indiana, 1972
- Lippincott, Horace Mather. *An Account of the People called Quakers in Germantown*, Philadelphia. (1922)
- Matlack, T. Chalkley. *Brief Historical Sketches concerning Friends' Meetings of the Past and Present with special reference to Philadelphia Yearly Meeting*, 1938, unpublished manuscript at Swarthmore College, Friends Historical Library
- McCracken, George E. *Penn's Colony: Genealogical and Historical Materials Relating to the Settlement of Pennsylvania: Volume 2. The Welcome Claimants: Proved, Disproved and Doubtful, With an Account of Some of Their Descendants.* Baltimore: Genealogical Publishing Company, 1970. This book is considered the standard reference on those individuals who were accepted as passengers with William Penn in 1682.
- Michener, Ezra. *A Retrospect of Early Quakerism; being extracts from the records of Philadelphia Yearly Meeting and the meetings composing it*, T. Ellwood Zell, Philadelphia, 1860
- Moore, John M., ed. *Friends in the Delaware Valley: Philadelphia Yearly Meeting, 1681-1981 (1981)* Myers, Albert Cook. *Immigration of the Irish Quakers into Pennsylvania, 1682-1750: with their early history in Ireland.* Swarthmore, Pennsylvania, 1902. **This book is on Ancestry.com.**
- Myers, Albert Cook. *Warrington Monthly Meeting of the Society of Friends), Warrington Township near Wellsville, York County, Pennsylvania.* York, Pa.: 1950. (Includes tombstone inscriptions.) **This book is on Ancestry.com.**
- Roberts, Clarence Vernon, comp. *Early Friends Families of Upper Bucks,* Pennsylvania. Philadelphia: the compiler, 1925
- Sheppard, Walter Lee, Jr. *Passengers and Ships Prior to 1684. Volume 1 of Penn's Colony: Genealogical and Historical Materials relating to the Settlement of Pennsylvania.* 1970. Reprint Bowie, Md., Heritage Books, Inc., 1996. This book is a definitive work on early passenger lists to the Delaware River.
- Watring, Anna Miller. *Bucks County Pennsylvania Church Records of 17th & 18th Centuries,* Vol 3, (Family Line Publications; Westminster MD) 1994

- Watring, Anna Miller. *Early Quaker Records of Philadelphia, Vols. I&II (1682-1800)*
- Wilson, Robert H. *Philadelphia Quakers, 1681-1981.* Philadelphia Yearly Meeting, 1981

The Dictionary of Quaker Biography

The Dictionary of Quaker Biography was compiled jointly by Friends House Library in London and Haverford College Quaker Collection. It consists of approximately 20,000 biographical entries on prominent British and American Friends from the 17th through the 20th centuries. There are two "original copies," one located at Haverford and the other at Friends House Library, London. Friends Historical Library at Swarthmore College has a photocopy of the Haverford "copy." For information about this excellent collection, go to this website: http://trilogy.bryn-mawr.edu/speccoll/dictionary/index.php/Digital_Dictionary_of_Quaker_Biography.

SOUTH CAROLINA

All available meeting records are in the Quaker Collection on Ancestry.com.

Finding Aids:

- Lucas, Silas Emmett, Rev. Jr. *Quakers in South Carolina: Wateree and Bush River, Dane Creek, Piney Grove and Charleston Meetings.* Greenville, South Carolina: Southern Historical Press, 1991
- Medlin, William F. *Quaker Families of South Carolina and Georgia.* Columbia?, SC: Ben Franklin Press, 1982

TENNESSEE

Some meeting records for this state are in the Quaker Collection on Ancestry.com. See North Carolina.

VIRGINIA

Some meeting records for this state are included in the Quaker Collection on Ancestry.com.

Finding Aids:

- Bell, James P. *Our Quaker Friends of Ye Olden Time being in part a Transcript of the Minute Books of Cedar Creek Meeting, Hanover County, and the South River Meeting, Campbell*

County, VA. 1905. Reprint, Baltimore: Genealogical Publishing Co., 1976

- Fawcett, Thomas H. "Quaker Migration from Pennsylvania and New Jersey to Hopewell Monthly Meeting, 1732-1759." *Bulletin of Friends' Historical Association.* No. 26, p. 102-108
- *Hopewell Friends History, 1734-1934, Frederick County, Virginia*, Records of Hopewell Monthly Meetings and Meetings Reporting to Hopewell, **GPC, 1993**
- **White, Miles, Jr.** *Early Quaker Records in Virginia*, **GPC, 1979**
- Worrall, Jay Jr. *The Friendly Virginians: America's First Quakers* Iberian Publishing
- Co., Athens, GA, 1994. This book reviews all of the meetings in Virginia, as well as many individuals.

Friends Reference Libraries and Historical Societies

In addition to the Quaker repositories previously listed, there are libraries and historical societies with microfilms and books about Quakers and Quaker records. Many of these resources are wonderful collections that will enhance a researcher's understanding of early Quaker ancestors. Some produce informative monthly publications and, for a small fee, members can purchase these publications. As you might expect, most of them are located in the geographical areas that had Quaker communities. Researchers should consider joining the historical or genealogical society in each of the counties where their Quaker ancestors lived. The information available is well worth any small annual membership fees.

This list is just a small representation of the many historical societies with Quaker collections in the United States.

UNITED STATES

Repository:	**Bucks County Historical Society**
Location:	84 S. Pine Street, Doylestown, PA 18901
Phone:	215-345-0210
Website:	http://www.mercermuseum.org

Repository:	**Burlington County Historical Society**
Location:	451 High Street, City of Burlington, NJ 08016
Phone:	609-386-4773

Website: http://www.burlingtoncountyhistoricalsociety.org/

Repository: **Chester County Historical Society**
Location: 225 N. High Street, West Chester, PA 19380
Phone: 610-692-4800
Website: http://www.chestercohistorical.org/

Repository: **Historical Society of Pennsylvania**
Location: 1300 Locust Street, Philadelphia, PA 19107
Phone: 215-732-6200
Website: http://www.hsp.org

Repository: **Indiana Historical Society**
Location: 450 W. Ohio Street, Indianapolis, IN 46202
Phone: 317-232-1882
Website: http://www.indianahistory.org

Repository: **Newberry Library**
Location: 60 W. Walton Street, Chicago, IL 60610
Phone: 312-255-3506
Website: http://www.newberry.org

Repository: **New York Genealogical & Biographical Society**
Location: 122 East 58th Street, New York, NY 10022
Phone: 212-755-8532
Website: http://newyorkfamilyhistory.org

Repository: **Ohio Genealogical Society**
Location: 713 South Main Street, Mansfield, OH 43211
Phone: 419-756-7294
Website: http://www.ogs.org

Repository: **Friends Historical Association**

Hosted at the Magill Library, Quaker Collection, at Haverford College, Haverford, PA. Membership in the Friends Historical Association is open to all who are interested in the Quaker heritage.

Location: 370 Lancaster Ave, Haverford, PA 19041

Phone: 610-896-1161

Website: http://www.haverford.edu/library/fha/welcome.html

Repository: **National Society of Descendants of Early Quakers, Founded in 1980**

This society produces an annual publication, *PLAIN LANGUAGE*, for its members.

Contact: Marlene Wilkinson, National Corresponding Clerk

Phone: 901-872-3575

Website: http://www.earlyquakers.org

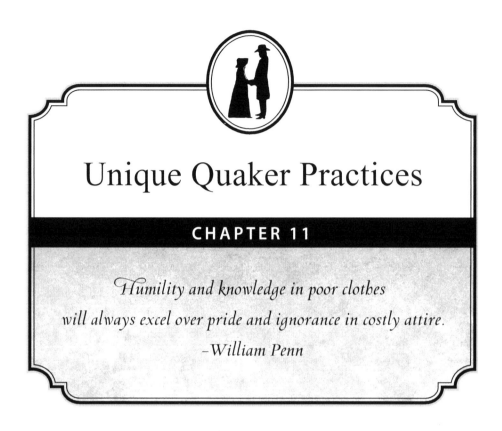

Unique Quaker Practices

CHAPTER 11

Humility and knowledge in poor clothes
will always excel over pride and ignorance in costly attire.
–William Penn

THIS CHAPTER EXPLAINS THE REASONING behind a variety of unique Quaker practices. Learning about Quaker ancestors does not include just their names and addresses. It also begs an understanding of their lives and insight into their most common practices. Not every member followed the practices outlined here, but most felt it was part of their Christian faith to do so.

Dress

Quakers were admonished to avoid fanciness in dress. Quaker women wore styles of the period, although probably not the latest fashions. "Of the best sort, but plain" was a common phrase. They used muted colors of grey, cream, and deep greens in fabrics of the day, such as silk and good quality wool. They avoided decorations and elements such as superfluous buttons, feathers, scarves, and the like. Friends felt that trendy fashions caused people to focus on themselves more than on their fellow human beings. Simple clothing made Quakers easily recognizable to society around them, particularly in the 18th and 19th Centuries.

George Fox admonished: "Friends, keep out of the vain fashions of the world; let not your eyes, minds, and spirits run after every fashion…for that will lead you from the solid life into unity with that spirit that leads to despair; but mind that which is sober and modest, and keep to your plain fashions…."

Book of Discipline—Instructions on How to Be a Disciple or Follower of Christ

Early Quakers did not agree with the Christianity of their day. They felt that the churches had forgotten the real Christ. After reading the Bible for themselves, they determined to go back to the early forms of Christianity, where Christ's words and the examples he set were the expected Christian standard. The earliest statement of this "discipline" was the *Epistle from the Meeting of Elders at Balby*, in 1656. This document was a list of 20 "advices" as to how Friends should conduct themselves; it was drafted

FIGURE 11-1: *Quaker dress was simple and tended to be modest and understated.*

following a meeting of prominent Quakers at Balby in Yorkshire and is seen by many as the platform of early Quaker thought. George Fox drafted a second book of advisements, again outlining what it meant to be a follower of Christ, addressing every aspect of an individual's life; it was produced following a meeting of leading Quakers in London in 1669.

When yearly meetings were created in America, each produced its own *Book of Discipline*, based on the earlier volumes from the London and Dublin Yearly Meetings. Each collection of advices regarding the Christian behavior of Quakers was a compilation of guidelines covering every aspect of Quaker life, from individual conduct and conversation, to proper management of meetings. (See sample list below)

Disciplines were revised according to changes in the beliefs and practices of Friends over

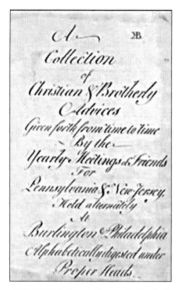

FIGURE 11-2: *Sample image of a Book of Discipline*

time, and each yearly meeting periodically reviewed and revised the printed guidelines accordingly. The contents of each yearly meeting's *Book of Discipline* were agreed on by seeking unity among its members at their annual conference. The process by which they made these changes is an interesting study in the methodology of most decision-making within the Quaker religion. Instead of voting, the authors (representatives from the monthly and quarterly meetings that were associated with each yearly meeting) attempted to gain a sense of God's will for the community. Each member of the writing group was expected to listen to promptings within themselves and to contribute it to the group for reflection and consideration. They were expected to listen to others' contributions carefully, in an attitude of seeking truth, rather than debate. This process, although tedious and lengthy, was thought to be the best way and was consistent with the intention that the books be based on evolving personal experience and "inner light" rather than on fixed creeds. The writings were not intended to represent strict rules but to be used as a source of guidance. Extracts from the book were often read aloud in Meetings for Worship, for the purpose of reflection.

The Philadelphia Yearly Meeting published its *Rules of Discipline of the Yearly Meeting of Friends Held in Philadelphia* in 1806, with advices on each of the main practices and testimonies, arranged in alphabetical order.

These are some of the topics they addressed:

Appeals	Convinced Persons
Arbitrations	Days and Times
Births and Burials	Defamation and Detraction
Books	Discipline and Meetings for Discipline
Certificates	Donations and Subscriptions
Charity and Unity	Family Visits
Civil Government	Gaming and Diversions
Conduct and Conversation	Law

Marriages

Meeting Houses

Meeting for Sufferings

Meetings for Worship

Memorials

Ministers and Elders

Moderation and Temperance

Negroes or Slaves

Oaths

Overseers

Parents and Children

Plainness

Poor

Priests' Wages; or Hireling Ministry

Queries

Queries for Meetings of Ministers and Elders

Schools

Scriptures of the Old and New Testaments

Stock

Taverns

Testimonies of Denial and Acknowledgments

Trade

War

Wills

Women's Meetings

Women's Quarterly Meetings

The Yearly Meeting of Women Friends

Yearly Meeting

LEARN MORE: You can access pages from the Philadelphia *Book of Discipline* of 1806 at: http://www.qhpress.org/texts/obod/index.html.

Weddings

A Quaker wedding ceremony was quiet, simple affair. There were no bridesmaids and no music. It was usually held during the mid-week silent Meeting for Worship, and was usually under the care of the bride's meeting, if the couple were not both members of the same meeting. There was no ring exchange. (Many Quaker couples never wore wedding rings, feeling that they were too ornate and ostentatious.) The bride usually wore a simple dress. At some point during the silence, the couple stood and exchanged their vows. Since there was no paid clergy, they were essentially marrying each other. Either then, or at the close of the meeting, the couple signed the marriage certificate and the entire certificate was read aloud to the attendees as part of the ceremony. The certificate was the only official marriage document and a copy was written into the records of the meeting, indicating that the marriage took place. There was no record of the marriage in either parish or civil records.

FIGURE 11-3: The Quaker wedding certificate is read aloud as part of the ceremony. (Author's wedding photo, 1974)

The early Quakers were given special legal dispensation that allowed them to legally marry their members, provided that both the man and woman were members. This dispensation began in England and continued in the Colonies. When a Quaker couple married, although there was no clergy present to officially declare it so, the verbal commitment to each other in the presence of God, their families, and their friends, was considered legally binding. The monthly meeting was legally responsible for making sure that everyone signed the wedding certificate as witnesses that the marriage took place. The meeting also assigned two members of the Overseers Committee to attend and report back to the monthly meeting so that the "accomplished" marriage could be recorded in the minutes. The marriage took place in a worship setting, because it was viewed as a religious commitment that the entire membership endorsed and supported. The exact text of the certificate and (in the early years) the names of all those in attendance were written into the meeting minutes, as proof in case there was ever a legal question. The married couples kept the certificates and often passed them down through generations. It was often the case that Quaker couples, when faced with the challenges of marriage, found renewed strength to persevere when viewing the signatures of all the family and friends who had witnessed and supported their wedding vows. (See Chapter 6, "Major Record Types," for more information about Quaker marriages.)

Plain Language

Early Quakers used what came to be called the "Plain language." In many languages, there is a familiar or informal form for the second-person pronoun ("you" in English). For Quakers, this familiarity was expressed by using "thee" or "thou" in place of "you." (For other language comparisons, think "tu" rather than "vous" in French and "tu" rather than "usted" in Spanish. In these examples, "thee" takes the place of "tu," and "thou"

FIGURE 11-4: All attendees sign the wedding certificate as legal witnesses.

takes the place of "vous" and "usted.") George Fox wanted to reform several verbal expressions in his day, "you" being one of them, as they appeared to convey flattery or to be idolatrous. He called on Quakers to depart from all vain customs of the world, which included various modes of speech. Fox adopted the use of Plain language for use with persons in *all* levels of society in an effort to avoid class distinction and acknowledge the equality of all people as children of God. He quietly used it in his own pattern of speech, and others followed his example. Over time, the

Plain language became the accepted way all Quakers spoke.

In defense of this peculiarity, William Penn wrote the following, "the word 'you' was first ascribed on the way of flattery, to proud Popes and Emperors, imitating the heathens in vain homage to their gods, thereby ascribing a plural honor to a single person; as if one Pope had been made up of many gods, and one Emperor of many men; for which reason 'you,' only to be addressed to many; became first spoken to one, It seemed the word 'thou' looked too lean and thin a respect; and therefore some, bigger that than they should be, would have a style suitable to their own ambition." While it is difficult in our day to understand how the use of the word "you" could ever have flattery attached to it, or how men could believe themselves to be elevated by others using that term in their presence, but history defines it as such.

Other Unique Language Practices

Quakers used given names when addressing people in written and verbal form. They rejected the words "Sir," "Madam," "Master," and "Mister" because their use at that time was considered a form of flattery derived from the papal and anti-Christian ages. They also rejected other terms commonly used in their day, such as "My Lord," "Your Excellency," "Your Grace," and "Your Honor." They felt that an individual could not court earthly honors by using flattering words and still have sufficient humility of mind and spirit to become a follower of Christ. Even in the letters that Fox sent to rulers of other nations, he wrote his remarks to them using their names without their titles.

Many Friends continued using Plain language for generations, and some still use it today, although the use of "thou" was discontinued and replaced with "thee" long ago. It is spoken this way, using "thee," "thy," and "thine" in place of "you," "your," and "yours." For example, you would say "*Thee* looks chilly!" "Can I get *thy* sweater?" "Is this blue sweater *thine*?"

Swearing of Oaths

In law, an affirmation is a solemn declaration permitted to those who conscientiously object to taking an oath and has exactly the same legal effect. Quakers had two strong arguments for affirming rather than swearing to take an oath. First, if you "swear to tell the truth and nothing but the truth," how is that different from what you were doing a few minutes ago, or yesterday? Quakers believed in speaking the truth at all times, so the act of swearing to tell the truth only in court or only in that setting, rather than in everyday life, would have implied a double standard.

Therefore, they chose to give an "affirmation", which to them meant continuing to tell the truth, just like they always did. The second argument resides in the Sermon on the Mount, when the Lord Jesus Christ instructed Christians to "swear not at all." The Quakers took this directive quite literally.

Schools

Quakers in America believed in education for all—men and women, rich and poor, black and white, slave and free. There were typically two types of schools for educating children from the elementary years through high school. The first type was the meeting school, where a meeting invited a schoolmaster (usually also a Quaker) to teach in the meeting house; the second type was the private school, which were held in buildings on private grounds, often with rooms for boarding students. There were countless numbers of both types of Quaker schools in the Colonies. Some of the private schools admitted only Quaker children and required the use of the Plain language and attendance at Meeting for Worship. Most meeting schools were open to all children and were less strict in regulations.

Some early Quakers used their personal funds to establish schools. Johns Hopkins, for instance, was a philanthropist from a Quaker family in Maryland who used his wealth to establish an orphanage, a hospital, a school of nursing, and eventually the medical school that holds his name today. Isaiah Williamson was another Quaker who saw a need and founded a school specifically for financially disadvantaged young men from farms outside Philadelphia. Through a deed of trust, he directed that the ideals of hard work, honesty, religious faith, and modest lifestyle be instilled in the students. He said that "in this country every able-bodied, healthy young man who has learned a good mechanical trade, and is truthful, honest, frugal, temperate, and industrious, is certain to succeed in life, and to become a useful and respected member of society." He provided this education free of charge to boys from all denominations.

Quaker Business Policies

Quakers had a distinct advantage in business, as their reputation for honesty and reliability ran parallel with their quest for justice, equality, and social reform. They were among the first business owners to set a firm price for goods. Bartering for price was the common practice, but Philadelphia Friends were encouraged by William Penn to decide on a fair price for goods and apply it to all buyers, regardless of their socioeconomic status. People who dealt with them appreciated the fact that they could trust Quaker businessmen, who needed to make a living but would not do it by taking advantage of customers. This kind of ethical approach gave Quaker retailers a competitive advantage over their rivals. Their reputation for honesty and reliability carried over into politics as Pennsylvania area Quakers were elected to governing positions for over 75 years, even though other groups moved into the area and the Quakers became a distinct minority.

A good example of the Quaker influence on business can be found in Cadbury Chocolate, one of several British firms founded by Quakers. In 1824, John Cadbury opened a grocer's shop in Birmingham, England. Among other things, he sold cocoa and drinking chocolate which he prepared himself using a pestle and mortar. The Cadbury manufacturing business was born in 1831, when John Cadbury decided to start producing on a commercial scale and bought a four-story warehouse nearby. When his sons George and Richard, also Quakers, took over running the business, they purchased land on the south side of Birmingham and built the village of Bournville for Cadbury workers and their families. It had homes with large garden areas, schools, and parks. They made provisions for pensions and, knowing that a healthy workforce was a productive workforce, the firm employed doctors and dentists to care for employees at a time when there was massive unemployment in Britain.

The perception of Quakers as being trustworthy producers of quality goods remains powerful, and their "brand" is sometimes exploited. For example, Quaker Oats Company, founded in the late 1800s, still uses the image of a traditionally dressed Quaker on its cereal boxes—despite never having any connection to the Quakers.

Twenty Top Businesses & Organizations with Quaker Origins

Amnesty International

Barclays Bank

Bethlehem Steel

Bradshaw's Railway Timetables (used throughout Britain, India & Europe)

Cadbury Chocolate

Carr's Biscuits

Clark's shoes

Cornell University

Greenpeace

Huntsman Steel Corp

Inman Shipping Lines

Johns Hopkins University

Lloyds Bank (now Lloyds TSB)

Queen City Oil Company, Toronto (is now Imperial Oil)

Robert Roberts's teas

Rowntree's Chocolates

Sony

Stockton & Darlington Railway

Waterford Crystal

Wharton School of Business

References and Suggested Reading

1. Clarkson, Thomas. *A Portraiture of Quakerism: Taken from a View of the Moral Education, Discipline, Peculiar Customs, Religious Principles, Political and Civil Economy, and Character, of the Society of Friends,* Indianapolis: Merrill & Field, 1870

2. Tolles, Frederick B. *Meeting House and Counting House: the Quaker Merchants of Colonial Philadelphia, 1682-1763.* New York: W.W. Norton & Co., Inc.,1948

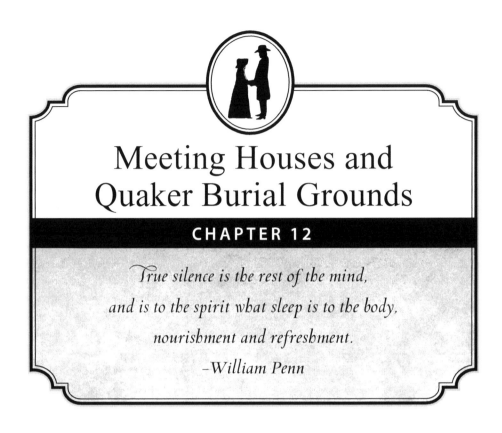

Meeting Houses and Quaker Burial Grounds

CHAPTER 12

True silence is the rest of the mind,
and is to the spirit what sleep is to the body,
nourishment and refreshment.

–William Penn

QUAKER MEETING HOUSES ARE STILL standing in towns and cities throughout the eastern and mid-western United States. They are distinct in style and appearance, and they serve as charming reminders of years long ago. Burial grounds were often part of the property and were not restricted to members only. This chapter will give you a better understanding of meeting houses, funerals, and the unusual headstones used in Quaker burial grounds.

Meeting Houses

Quaker meeting houses are one of the last remaining vestiges of the early Quakers, still visible today.

Why and How Meeting Houses Were Built

As mentioned in previous chapters, George Fox's followers did not believe that meeting for worship had to occur in any special place. They based their gatherings on the Biblical scripture from

FIGURE 12-1: Quaker Meeting House - Exterior

Matthew 18:20, which states, "For where two or three have gathered together in my name, there am I in the midst of them." Hence, a Meeting for Worship could take place anywhere, and early Quakers often met for worship outdoors or in public buildings. When the sect began to grow, there became a need for buildings to house their meetings.

The use of the term, "meeting house" was purposeful. Fox determined from the New Testament that the word "church" actually referred to the body of people who make up the worshipping community; hence, Quakers do not use the word "church" to refer to the bricks and mortar of a building. Fox referred to places of worship that had steeples as "steeple houses," and, those that did not, as "meeting houses."

The hallmark of a meeting house is plainness, an absence of any outward symbols or ostentations. When given the opportunity to design and construct their own places of meeting, Friends infused simplicity in the planning, design, and construction of the buildings. Seen as an improvement over the small, cottage-style meeting houses built in England, the Colonial meeting houses had spacious interiors with equal provision made for both the women's and men's sides. Men and women worshipped together, though they sat on separate sides of the meeting houses until the early 20th century.

Meeting houses built in a traditional style usually had two meeting rooms: a large one for the main meeting for worship, and another smaller one where the women's business meeting was held. Meeting houses usually had long, wooden benches for seating, all facing toward the center of the room, often with a gallery above for extra seating. They usually had high windows so that worshippers could not see the activities of the outside world while meditating. The meeting house was a place for Friends to withdraw from the world, to renew themselves each Sunday though meditation, prayer, and fellowship. As they sat in quiet meditation, early Quakers could usually hear the ticking of the old grandfather clock in the corner and feel the heat from the wood stove in the center of the room.

Meeting houses were built to last and were designed for large congregations, of which there were over 200 just in the Philadelphia area alone. In 1891, a visitor to the Bucks County area of Pennsylvania, after having seen several of the large, stone meeting houses, commented: "A few things are noticeable in all the meeting houses in this section: (1) they are all capacious and evidently intended for large congregations; (2) they were honestly built, and built to last, being very solid structures of stone, with the evident expectancy that the Society of Friends had come to stay; and (3) the evident taste and refinement of those early Friends, evinced in the neat paneling of the shutters and trimming of the woodwork in the building. They must have been quite as tasteful as the dwellings of that early day."

Some of the early meeting houses were of log construction and have burned or been taken down. But a drive around the eastern counties of Pennsylvania will reveal many charming, old, stone buildings still standing after 200 years. If you would like to take a peek at some meeting houses, visit: http://freepages.genealogy.rootsweb.ancestry.com/~paxson/graphics-pax/mtghse.html.

Another wonderful resource for meeting house photos is the website for Haverford's Quaker Collection: http://www.haverford.edu/library/special/collections/quaker/meeting_houses.php.

Funerals

Early Quakers tended to have very simple funerals. A funeral was called a "memorial service" or sometimes, "A Meeting for Worship in thanksgiving for the grace of God, as shown in the life of _____". A Quaker funeral was usually held in a meeting house and was a silent Meeting

FIGURE 12-2: Benches all faced inward, instead of toward an altar or pulpit.

for Worship, wherein those who were close to or related to the deceased gathered to honor and remember him or her. Some might share a memory with the congregation, though there was usually no eulogy given. The service often began with an explanation by the Elders of what would happen during the meeting, because it was assumed that a number of mourners were not Quakers and would not know the Quaker customs. Then everyone sat in silent meditation. A Quaker funeral was not a somber affair but rather a celebration of the life that was lived. In honor of this fact, Quakers did not wear black as a symbol of mourning. There was no prescribed mourning period or memorial events for Quakers.

Usually, there was no wake or viewing before the funeral, nor a casket or urn at the funeral. The goal of a Quaker funeral was simply to thank God for the life that had been lived and to help mourners feel God's love.

Burial Grounds

Quaker burial grounds are an area where there was considerable variation within common practices that varied from one yearly meeting to another. There was usually a funeral committee, made up of members of the meeting who had oversight of funerals and made necessary arrangements for the burial. Historically, the deceased were buried in the next available lot, although some meetings allowed families to be buried in nearby lots. This practice was not the norm.

FIGURE 12-3: *Quaker Burial Grounds were kept simple with headstones of similar shape and height, in order to elimate any contrast between rich and poor.*

Most meetings were liberal in allowing individuals of reduced circumstances, including American Indians and slaves, to be buried in the burial grounds; although, as burial grounds filled up, more restrictions were imposed on burials of non-Quakers. Early Quakers did not allow public displays of wealth or position in their cemeteries. For this reason, you will not find large stones or epitaphs in a Quaker burial ground; stones were kept small and of a uniform shape and size.

Per the 1717 Quaker *Book of Discipline*: ".... in each particular burial ground, such uniformity is preserved in respect to the materials, size, form and wording of the stones, as well as in the mode of placing them, as may effectually guard against any distinction being made in that place between the rich and the poor."

Here are some other details to remember about Quaker burial grounds:

- If there were any stones, they only provided the names of the deceased, their ages, and their dates of death.

- The earliest Quaker burial grounds were simple fields of unmarked stone, in keeping with the discipline of simplicity.

- The Philadelphia and Ohio Yearly Meetings did not permit tombstones until the end of the 1800s.

- Not all individuals who were buried there are Quakers.

- Not all Quakers were buried in Quaker burial grounds.

- Some meetings did not keep careful records of the persons buried in their lots; they relied instead on the memories of their members to know where to dig the next lot

- Some meetings kept meticulous records of burials in plot maps.

- For a description and maps of "Quaker Burial Grounds in Philadelphia from 1683 to Present," visit http://www.swarthmore.edu/library/friends/philaburials3.htm.

References and Suggested Reading

Haviland, R. S. "Visits and Meetings in Bucks County" *Friends Intelligencer* 48:12, Mar. 21, 1891, p. 187

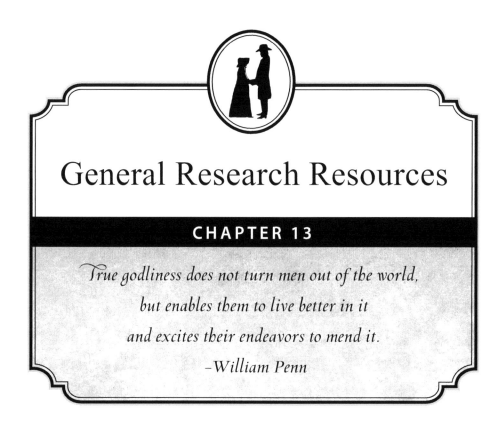

General Research Resources

CHAPTER 13

True godliness does not turn men out of the world,
but enables them to live better in it
and excites their endeavors to mend it.

–William Penn

THIS CHAPTER FOCUSES ON SOME of the essentials, such as: hiring a professional to help with research, annual genealogy conferences and seminars, and Quaker-related societies.

Hiring a Professional Genealogy Researcher

Would you like help deciding the best plan for research, or do you want to join a lineage society and need help with your application? Maybe you could use assistance translating records, organizing documents and photos, or planning a family reunion? Professional genealogy researchers can help you with all of these tasks and more.

Hiring a professional genealogist is an excellent way to discover your family roots. An experienced researcher can be a great resource, whether you're facing a challenging research problem, lacking the skills or the time to conduct research yourself, or having difficulty with travel. These guidelines can help you find a researcher in the area in which you wish to conduct research. They can also save you time and money.

Keep the following tips in mind when hiring a professional researcher:

- **Fees:** Many professional researchers charge an hourly rate plus additional fees for travel and copying costs. Researchers usually ask for a deposit up front that will be retained until the research is completed.

- **Credentials:** Many professional genealogists have obtained a higher level of education as well as certification by one or both of the two accrediting bodies for professional research-ers. If a genealogist does not have credentials, ask him or her for references from past clients. Also inquire about other education and training that he or she may have received, either historical or genealogical, and about his or length of experience in the field. Finally, ask about his or her memberships to genealogical societies. Certain societies, such as the Association of Professional Genealogists, require their members to sign a code of ethics.

- **Expectations:** Discuss what kind of work you want done on your family lines. If you are uncertain, the researcher you have chosen should be happy to help you develop a focused plan. You may choose to contact several researchers so that you can compare fees and current client loads before you select your professional.

- **Communication:** Many research projects can take an extended length of time, depending on how far back you wish to trace your family tree. Discuss realistic time expectations regarding how soon the researcher will be able to work on your particular family and how often you can expect to receive a report on his or her findings. Open communication with your researcher is a benefit to both of you. However, keep in mind that a steady stream of emailed questions from you can slow down the research.

- **Location:** Do you need a researcher in England or one in the United States, who has access to the records at the courthouse in your county of interest? You can select from a list of people who perform research in the country or county of interest to you. (See "Association of Professional Genealogists (APG).")

The *Guide to Hiring a Professional Genealogy Researcher* is an excellent resource that covers several other aspects of hiring a professional. It is available at:

http://familysearch.org/learn/wiki/en/Hiring_a_Professional_Researcher.

Professional Genealogy Associations

The following professional genealogy associations have thousands of members who do professional research. Each association requires members to sign a code of ethics that applies to providing professional family history research for clients. This fact will help to protect you, should any issues arise.

Association of Professional Genealogists (APG)

The Association of Professional Genealogists has more than 1400 members who each have his or her own specialties in family history research. Many members of the association are either certified or accredited, and many have educational backgrounds and years of experience in professional genealogy.

Website: http://www.apgen.org

APG's online membership directory allows you to search for specialists by:
- Geographical area
- Research specialty (for example, American Indian, adoption, translations, etc.)
- State and province
- Country of residence

Board for Certification of Genealogists (BCG)

The Board for Certification of Genealogists is an independent certifying body. The BCG certifies genealogists who have met a certain level of competence in genealogical research. Its online directory lists certified genealogists and their specialties.

Website: http://www.bcgcertification.org

International Commission for the Accreditation of Professional Genealogists (ICAPGen)

This organization tests genealogists in specific localities. It offers an online directory of accredited genealogists.

Website: http://www.icapgen.org

Conferences and Seminars

There are several conferences each year where you can take classes about family history.

Rootstech

The largest annual genealogy conference is held in Salt Lake City in February. Many of the sessions during this three-day event are broadcast online, and most are archived. Visit its website for more information.

Website: https://rootstech.org/about/

Federation of Genealogical Societies

This group holds an annual conference that includes great lectures on Internet genealogy, record sources, and methodology. There are courses for all levels of experience.

Website: http://www.fgs.org

National Archives and Records Administration (NARA)

Most of the 13 NARA regional offices offer Saturday workshops that feature several different classes. They are usually free and open to anyone who is interested in learning about genealogical research, both online and while using original records from the National Archives.

Check the calendar of events each month to see which classes are being offered in each location.

Website: http://www.archives.gov/research/genealogy/events/

National Genealogical Society (NGS)

NGS holds an annual conference that includes talks on methodology, records, the Internet, and more. The NGS also offers home-study and online courses on the topics of beginning genealogy and census records. Visit its website for more information.

National Genealogical Society
3108 Columbia Pike, Suite 300
Arlington, VA 22204-4370
Website: http://www.ngsgenealogy.org

Brigham Young University

Brigham Young University (BYU), located in Provo, UT, hosts two annual genealogy conferences: the BYU Computerized Genealogy Conference (March) and the BYU Genealogy and Family History Conference (July). These conferences are sponsored by the LDS Family History Library, BYU History Department, BYU Center for Family History and Genealogy, and the BYU Division of Continuing Education. Speakers are nationally recognized for their expertise in family history.

BYU Conferences and Workshops

136 Harman Continuing Education Building

Provo, UT 84602-1516

Website: http://ce.byu.edu

BYU also offers a Bachelor of Arts degree, as well as a certification program, in family history and genealogy. The BYU courses are taught by professional genealogists and historians. The certification program can help a person prepare for BCG certification or accreditation through ICAPGen.

Brigham Young University

History Department

2130 JFSB

Provo, UT 84602-6707

Website: http://saas.byu.edu/catalog/2013-2014ucat/departments/History/FamHistoryCert.php

Repeat Performance

Even if you can't make it to any of these conferences, you can still learn in the comfort of your own home. Repeat Performance sells tapes of genealogy conferences, among others. Visit the company's website and peruse its genealogy section; you may be surprised at how many talks on tape are available.

Audiotapes.com

c/o Repeat Performance

2911 Crabapple Lane

Hobart, IN 46324

Website: http://www.audiotapes.com

Quaker Societies

The Welcome Society

This society aims to perpetuate the memory of the Quakers who came to America with William Penn and to bring together the descendants of these travelers. Currently, the membership is composed of descendants of only those ancestors who traveled with fellow Quakers to America in 1682. This includes 22 ships and 23 crossings of the Atlantic.

Website: http://www.welcomesociety.org

Quaker Family History Society

Membership is open to anyone who is interested in the history of British or Irish Quakers. This society distributes a publication three times a year and holds bi-annual meetings in London.

Website: http://www.qfhs.co.uk/

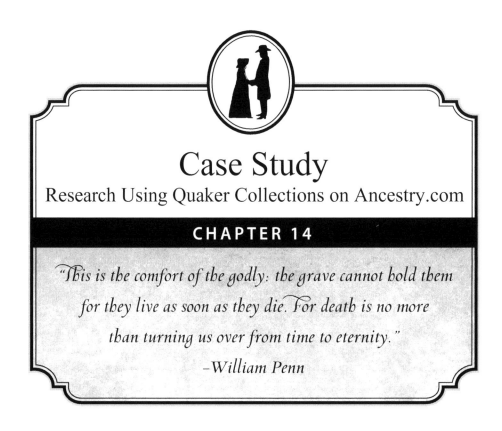

Case Study
Research Using Quaker Collections on Ancestry.com

CHAPTER 14

"This is the comfort of the godly: the grave cannot hold them for they live as soon as they die. For death is no more than turning us over from time to eternity."
—William Penn

THIS CHAPTER PRESENTS A SMALL research project and analysis, using three of the databases in the Quaker Collection on Ancestry.com:

1. U.S., Hinshaw Index to Selected Quaker Records, 1680–1940

2. U.S. and Canada, Quaker Monthly Meeting Historical Data, 1671–2010

3. U.S., Quaker Meeting Records, 1681–1994

The Hinshaw Index to Selected Quaker Records, 1680-1940 is an excellent resource for Quaker researchers, especially when they gain a level of comfort in using them. Together we will research one family, using both the Hinshaw Index (number one on the list above) and original Quaker Meeting records (number three on the list above), while we attempt to construct the context of their lives in a given time period. We will use the Monthly Meetings Index (number two above) to learn details about specific meetings. This will become clearer as we move through the exercise. We will move slowly and methodically, and it may be helpful to re-read this chapter a few times until you get more comfortable with the process. Then you can start creating shortcuts for yourself.

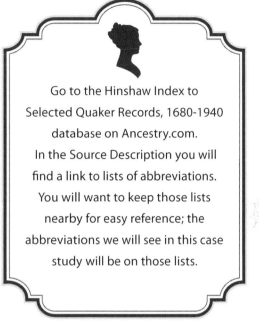

Go to the Hinshaw Index to Selected Quaker Records, 1680-1940 database on Ancestry.com. In the Source Description you will find a link to lists of abbreviations. You will want to keep those lists nearby for easy reference; the abbreviations we will see in this case study will be on those lists.

Three databases in the Quaker Collection on Ancestry.com were created from the final results of the Hinshaw abstraction project which was initiated in the 1930s and essentially ended with Hinshaw's death in 1947. The Encyclopedia has been used for decades by Quaker researchers. Some explanation about the scope of these databases will help to set clear expectations as to their contents:

1. The *Encyclopedia of American Quaker Genealogy, Vol I–VI, 1607–1977* (not used in this case study) is a valuable compendium of vital facts relating to a small percentage of American Quakers. *But Hinshaw's collection is not a list of all Quakers in the United States.* Hinshaw was only able to publish six volumes before his death. These six volumes contain only a fraction of the total meetings.

2. The *Hinshaw Index to Selected Quaker Records, 1680-1940* (used in this case study) contains thousands of names, but according to the Friends Historical Library at Swarthmore College, *the majority of Friends' meeting minutes were never abstracted* and will not be found in

either of the Hinshaw collections. In this database, as well as the Surname index below in number three, Hinshaw's teams were only able to complete the work of extracting meeting minutes for 300 meetings in 17 states, and there have been close to 2000 meetings.

3. The *U.S., Surname Index to Quaker Records* database contains a cross-index to *Hinshaw's Index to Selected Quaker Records, 1640-1940*. It is a list of surnames found in Hinshaw's Index of 300 meetings (see Number Two above), and each name is followed by a list of meetings in which that surname appears in the collection. You may find that it is worthwhile checking the list to see where your ancestor's surname appears; it may offer just the clue you need to continue your research.

Remember that the Hinshaw Index Cards are an abstraction; whenever possible, the original records from which these were abstracted should be consulted, both for verification and to look for more detail. Many monthly meeting records were placed on microfilm years ago. Those films were digitized by Ancestry.com and the images now appear in the *U.S., Quaker Meeting Records, 1681–1994* database. However, some records were never filmed, because they were lost or were still in the custody of their local meeting.

Case Study

We have chosen the family of David and Elizabeth Parry for this project. Throughout this narrative, we will expand the details found in the abbreviations and put all the details from the cards into sentences. Refer to the images and your list of abbreviations as we go through the steps.

1. Card #1

The first card contains the following information, which has been abridged from the original meeting minutes:

On 26 May 1795 (*date in upper left corner*) in the Philadelphia Northern District Monthly Meeting ("*PNDP*" *in upper left corner*), David Parry, his wife Elizabeth, and their

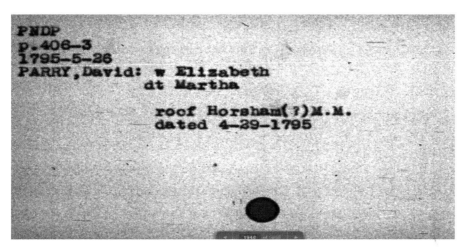

FIGURE 14-1: *from Hinshaw Index to Selected Quaker Records, 1680–1940.*

daughter Martha were received on a certificate from (*"rocf"*) Horsham Monthly Meeting. The certificate was dated 29 April 1795.

We interpret this to mean that the Parry family left Horsham, PA, around the end of April 1795 and settled in Philadelphia sometime in May of the same year. It is inferred that, upon arrival, they submitted their certificate to the new monthly meeting at the end of May, requesting membership there. We can assume that they were members "in good standing" in Horsham (their previous meeting), or they would not have been given a certificate. We would want to locate the original meeting minutes, both in the Horsham Monthly Meeting and the Philadelphia Northern District Monthly Meeting minutes, to see if there are any other details.

TIP 1: If you are unsure of the physical location of a meeting, use the Ancestry.com database entitled *U.S. and Canada, Quaker Monthly Meeting Historical Data, 1671-2010.* In this instance, we learn that Horsham Monthly Meeting is in Horsham, Montgomery County, PA, and the Philadelphia Northern District Monthly Meeting is in Philadelphia, at the intersection of 6th Street and Noble Street. (See both images below; they are from the *U.S. and Canada, Quaker Monthly Meeting Historical Data, 1671-2010.*)

North America, Quaker Monthly Meetings Index, 1671-2010	
Meeting Name:	Philadelphia, Northern District
Latest Yearly Meeting:	Philadelphia (Orthodox) Yearly Meeting
State or Province:	Pennsylvania
County:	Philadelphia
Physical Location:	Philadelphia 19123, 6Th and Noble
Records Known Extant:	Haverford: Minutes 1772-1914, Women Minutes 1772-1914, Births 1754-1884, Deaths 1772-1884, Memb 1796-1850, 1885-1914, Removals 1773-1914, Memb Transfers 1772-1820, Marriages 1772-1907
Where Records are Kept:	Haverford. Mf Swarthmore. Lds 20473-76, 384860
Comments:	Informal Hinshaw Transcripts, Pennsylvania Quaker Monthly Meeting Records Vol 7, From Selby Publishing (1990), Http://WwwSelbypubCom/PaHtm
Date Granted:	03 Aug 1772
Date of First Meeting:	24 Nov 1772
Date Laid Down:	May 1914
Date of Last Meeting:	22 Jun 1910
Former Meeting Names:	North Street (Informally)
Affiliations:	Philadelphia Quarterly Meeting
Subordinates:	Green Street Pm 1814/12-1816
Before and After:	Pm 1772-1914Bef From Philadelphia Monthly Meeting Attached To Philadelphia Monthly Meeting (Orthodox)
Records Website:	View Website
Another Website:	View Website

FIGURE 14-2: Meeting Name: Philadelphia Northern District. Ancestry.com. U.S. and Canada, Quaker Monthly Meeting Historical Data, 1671-2010. Original data: Hill, Thomas C., Monthly Meetings in North America: A Quaker Index. Earlham College, Richmond, Indiana.

North America, Quaker Monthly Meetings Index, 1671-2010	
Meeting Name:	Horsham
Latest Yearly Meeting:	Philadelphia Yearly Meeting
State or Province:	Pennsylvania
County:	Montgomery
Physical Location:	Horsham 19044, Meetinghouse Rd. and S.R. 611
Website:	View Website
Records Known Extant:	Swarthmore: Minutes 1782-1954, Women Minutes 1782-1793, 1819-1885, Marriages 1782-1953, Removals 1783-1940, Births 1713-1901, Deaths 1768-1889, Memb 1713-1947, Memb Transfers 1880-1940, Burials 1718-1968, M and E 1786-1944
Where Records are Kept:	Swarthmore Mf Haverford. Lds 20400, -16, -63, 383525
Comments:	Bound James E Hazard Complete-Name Genealogical Abstracts At Friends Historical Library, Swarthmore, Pa
Date Granted:	05 Aug 1782
Date of First Meeting:	29 Aug 1782
Date Laid Down:	Active
Branches:	Hicksite 29 Aug 1827 - 1955 Merger
Affiliations:	Philadelphia Quarterly Meeting Until 06 Feb 1786; Abington Quarterly Meeting After 04 May 1786
Subordinates:	Byberry Pm Until 1810Upper Dublin Pm 1816-1941Warminster Pm 1841-1953
Before and After:	Pm 1717-1959 From Abington Monthly Meeting

FIGURE 14-3: Meeting Name: Horshsam. Ancestry.com. U.S. and Canada, Quaker Monthly Meeting Historical Data, 1671-2010. Original data: Hill, Thomas C., Monthly Meetings in North America: A Quaker Index. Earlham College, Richmond, Indiana.

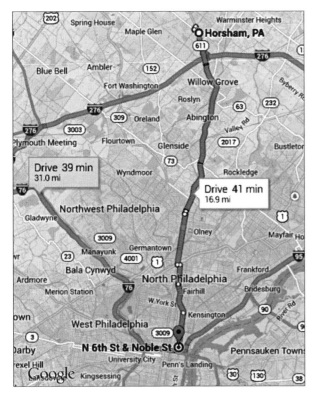

TIP 2: Now that we have the locations, we can chart them on a map.

FIGURE 14-4: google.com/maps

It appears that Horsham is about 17 miles north of Philadelphia.

2. Card #2

The second card contains the following information, abridged from the original meeting minutes:

On 28 May 1799, David Parry, his wife Elizabeth, and their children Martha, Jacob, and Samuel were granted a certificate to Buckingham Monthly Meeting from the Philadelphia Northern District Monthly Meeting.

Once again, we consult the *U.S. and Canada, Quaker Monthly Meetings Index, 1671–2010* database to find out where Buckingham Monthly Meeting is located.

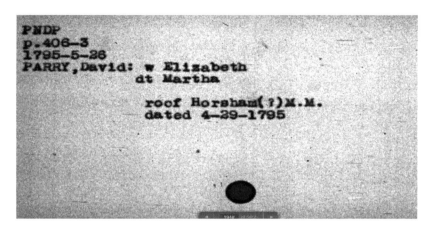

FIGURE 14-5: from Hinshaw Index to Selected Quaker Records, 1680–1940.

North America, Quaker Monthly Meetings Index, 1671-2010	
Meeting Name:	Buckingham
Latest Yearly Meeting:	Philadelphia Yearly Meeting
State or Province:	Pennsylvania
County:	Bucks
Physical Location:	Lahaska 18931, 5684 York Rd., Rte. 202 At Rte. 263
Latitude:	40.34592° N
Longitude:	075.03694° W
Website:	View Website
Records Known Extant:	Swarthmore: Minutes 1720-1966, Women Minutes 1722-1891, Births and Deaths 1699-1815, Marriages 1721-1947, Removals 1778-1957, Births 1742-1920, Burials 1930, Deaths 1772-1936, M and E 1787-1815, 1867-1928
Where Records are Kept:	Swarthmore. Mf Lds 20709, 172827-28, 388577-79
Date Granted:	24 Nov 1720
Date of First Meeting:	06 Dec 1720
Date Laid Down:	Active
Branches:	Hicksite 03 Sep 1827 - 1955
Affiliations:	Bucks Quarterly Meeting
Subordinates:	Plumstead Pm 1731-1867; Solebury Pm 1806-1811; Wrightstown Pm 1724/12-1734; Plumstead Worship 1969-2002; In 1752 Meetinghouse
Before and After:	Pm 1705-1955 From Falls Monthly Meeting
Local Related Histories:	Anna Miller Watring, Bucks County, Pennsylvania Church Records Of The 17Th and 18Th Centuries, Volume 3, Pp 141-191 (1994)
Records Website:	View Website

FIGURE 14-6: Meeting Name: Buckingham. Ancestry.com. U.S. and Canada, Quaker Monthly Meeting Historical Data, 1671-2010. Original data: Hill, Thomas C., Monthly Meetings in North America: A Quaker Index. Earlham College, Richmond, Indiana.

FIGURE 14-7: google.com/maps

According to the entry for Buckingham Meeting, it is in Lahaska, Bucks County, PA, about 30 miles north of Philadelphia.

We want to check the original minutes for the date that the Parry family settled in the Lahaska area. Because Buckingham Monthly Meeting was not included in the Hinshaw project, we will need to find it in the *U.S., Quaker Meeting Records, 1681–1994* database. We enter "David Parry" into the name fields, and add "Bucks County, PA" in the location box, which will help to narrow the results.

View Record	David Parry	Miscellaneous	3 Oct 1795	Bucks, Pennsylvania	
View Record	David Parry	Admittance	1 Jul 1799	Bucks, Pennsylvania	
View Record	David Parry	Admittance	1 Jul 1799	Bucks, Pennsylvania	
View Record	David Parry Jr	Removal	6 Apr 1801	Bucks, Pennsylvania	
View Record	David Parry	Removal	5 Oct 1801	Bucks, Pennsylvania	

FIGURE 14-8: Results page: "David Parry" in "Bucks County, PA". Ancestry.com. U.S., Quaker Meeting Records, 1681–1994. [database online]

Since the Parry family left Philadelphia in May 1799, the admittance entry for 1 Jul 1799 is the likely minute page that we are seeking.

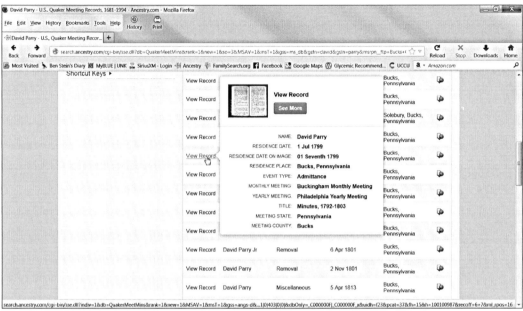

FIGURE 14-9: *Results page: "David Parry" in "Bucks County, PA". Ancestry.com. U.S., Quaker Meeting Records, 1681–1994. [database online]*

An easy way to see if you want to open any link on the results page is to hover your mouse over the phrase "View Record." When this is done, the details of the entry will pop up for easy reference. Given that the Parry family reportedly left Philadelphia at the end of May 1799, this entry may be the one we want. Click the "See More" button to view the original meeting minute.

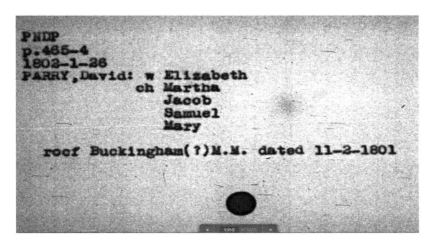

FIGURE 14-10: *Entry from Buckingham Women's Meeting Minutes. Ancestry.com. U.S., Quaker Meeting Records, 1681–1994. [database online]*

From this entry in the Buckingham Women's Meeting Minutes, it appears that we have selected the appropriate entry and it appears that are still researching the same family. Quaker families used similar given names, so take the time to verify that you are still researching the correct family!

3. Card #3

The Parry family has added a child, Mary, and it appears that they moved from Buckingham Monthly Meeting back to Philadelphia Northern District Monthly Meeting. The card reads:

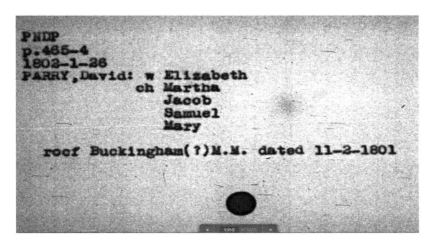

FIGURE 14-11: *from Hinshaw Index to Selected Quaker Records, 1680–1940.*

On 26 January 1802, David Parry, his wife Elizabeth, and their four children were received on a certificate from ("*rocf*") Buckingham Monthly Meeting by the Philadelphia Northern District Monthly Meeting. The certificate granted by the Buckingham Monthly Meeting was dated 2 Nov 1801.

The date [*11-2-1801*] gives us the clue we need to locate that entry in the Buckingham Monthly Meeting minutes. We return to the *U.S., Quaker Meeting Records, 1681–1994* database and search again under "David Parry" in "Bucks County, PA".

We will click on "View Record" for the second entry dated 2 Nov 1801, since that date matches the date on the card.

View Record	David Parry	Removal	5 Oct 1801	Bucks, Pennsylvania
View Record	David Parry	Removal	2 Nov 1801	Bucks, Pennsylvania
View Record	David Parry Jr	Removal	6 Apr 1801	Bucks,

FIGURE 14-12: *Results page: "David Parry" in "Bucks County, PA". Ancestry.com. U.S., Quaker Meeting Records, 1681–1994. [database online]*

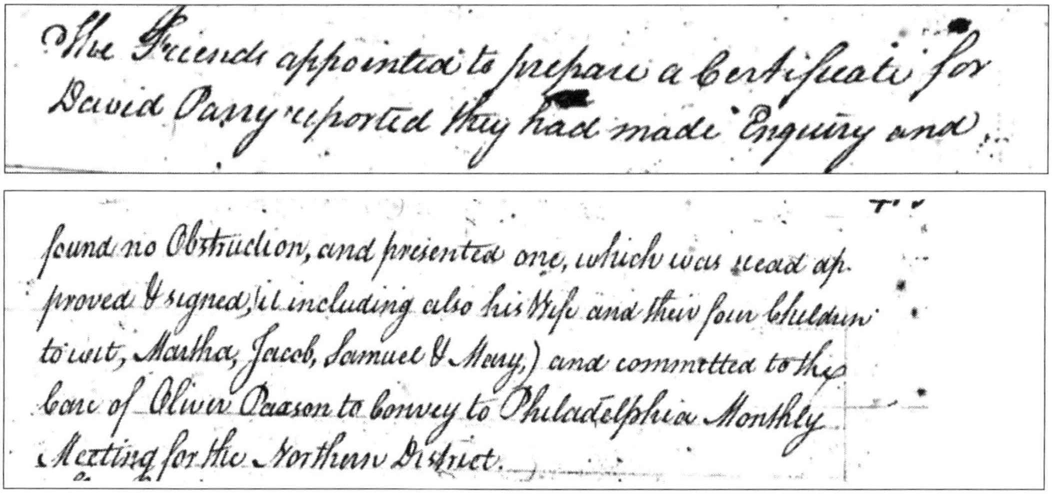
The Friends appointed to prepare a Certificate for David Parry reported they had made Enquiry and found no Obstruction, and presented one, which was read ap-proved & signed, (it including also his Wife and their four Children to wit, Martha, Jacob, Samuel & Mary,) and committed to the Care of Oliver Paxson to Convey to Philadelphia Monthly Meeting for the Northern District.

FIGURE 14-13: *Original entry from Buckingham Monthly Meeting minutes. Ancestry.com. U.S., Quaker Meeting Records, 1681–1994. [database online]*

Let's check the Hinshaw Index cards again to see if the Parry family appears in the minutes again. Some families rarely appear because they didn't need to request a certificate to move, or permission to get married, or for a burial in the meeting burial grounds. A quick search will tell us if they appear again. And we find another card.

3. Card #4

This card reveals that David Parry died at age 27 and was buried in Philadelphia on 17 July 1802. Let's see if we can find the original entry in the minute book.

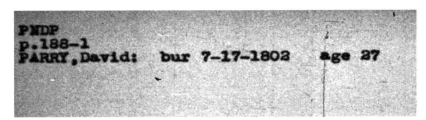

FIGURE 14-15: from Hinshaw Index to Selected Quaker Records, 1680–1940.

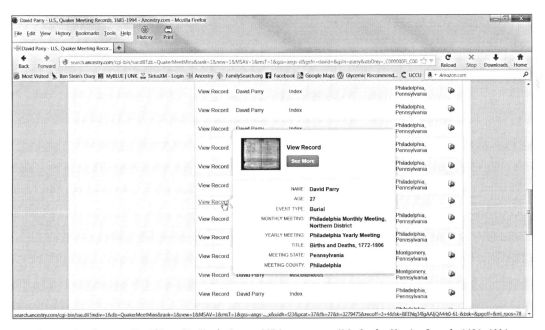

FIGURE 14-15: Results page: "David Parry" in "Bucks County, PA". Ancestry.com. U.S., Quaker Meeting Records, 1681–1994. [database online]

We find that there are dozens of entries in the U.S., Quaker Meeting Records, 1681–1994 database for David Parry (it is a common name), but if we scroll down we find an entry for a burial. Hovering our mouse over "view record", we can see some of the detail. Now it is time to click on "See More" and view the old record.

This entry is from the *Register of Births and Deaths for the Philadelphia Monthly Meeting, Northern District*, for July in the year 1802. David Parry is the fourth entry.

FIGURE 14-16: Register of Births and Deaths for the Philadelphia Monthly Meeting, Northern District. Ancestry.com. U.S., Quaker Meeting Records, 1681–1994.[database online]

5. Card #5

The next card I found for the Parry family indicates that about 10 months after David's death, Elizabeth planned to leave the Philadelphia Monthly Meeting, Northern District. She requested and was granted a certificate to ("*gct*") Horsham Monthly Meeting for herself and three children:

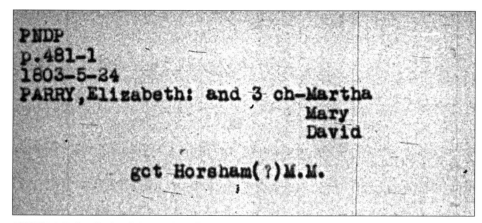

FIGURE 14-17: from Hinshaw Index to Selected Quaker Records, 1680–1940.

Martha, Mary, and David. David? That's a new name. Did she have another child after her husband died? There are no disciplinary actions taken against her recorded in the minutes, which leads us to believe that David's birth was legitimate.

But an issue has arisen: Why don't Samuel and Jacob appear on the card?

6. Card #6

Performing another search in the *Hinshaw Index to Quaker Records, 1680–1940*, this time using the name of Jacob Parry, we find this card. It appears that two of Elizabeth's young children, Jacob and Samuel, went to Abington Monthly Meeting, while she and the other children went

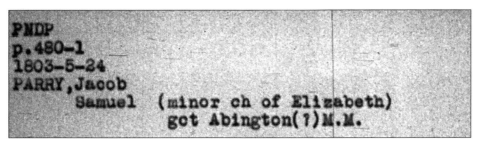

FIGURE 14-18: from Hinshaw Index to Selected Quaker Records, 1680–1940.

to Horsham Monthly Meeting.

Several questions may arise based on these new facts. Why would the children go there alone, almost 10 miles from their mother? Did she have family there?

1. A look into the *U.S., Quaker Meeting Records, 1681–1994* searching for Elizabeth Parry in the Horsham Monthly Meeting minutes reveals that on the 5th month 27 1807, an Elizabeth Parry moves from the Horsham Monthly Meeting to the Abington Monthly Meeting.

Question to ask ourselves: Is this our Elizabeth Parry?

Answer: Elizabeth Parry was a fairly common name with dozens of entries in the minutes, so we can't be sure that this is the Elizabeth we are tracking without more research into the minutes of the Abington Monthly Meeting. Our Elizabeth had several minor children whose names should have been listed on her certificate. Unless something happened to them and she was moving alone, this may not be *our* Elizabeth Parry.

The image below is from the original minutes of the Horsham Monthly Meeting. The clerk copied all of the text into the meeting minute book, as was the custom. It is a bit difficult to read, so I placed the transcription is beside it.

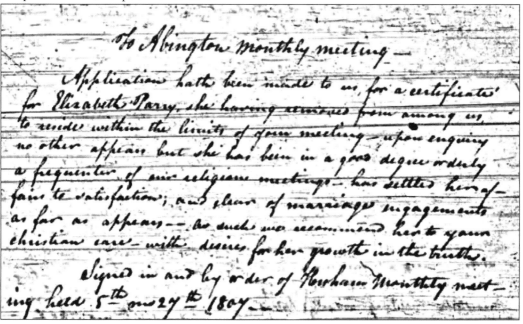

FIGURE 14-19: *Entry from original minutes of the Horsham Monthly Meeting. Ancestry.com. U.S., Quaker Meeting Records, 1681–1994. [database online]*

To Abington Monthly Meeting

Application hath been made to us, for a certificate for Elizabeth Parry, she having removed from among us to reside within the limits of your Meeting, upon inquiry no other appears but she has been in a good degree orderly; a frequenter of our religious Meetings, has settled her affairs to satisfaction, and clear of marriage engagements as far as appears, as such we recommend her to your Christian care with desires for her growth in the truth.

Signed in and by order of Horsham Monthly Meeting held 5 mo. 27 1807.

FIGURE 14-20: *Transcription of Certificate of Removal granted to Elizabeth Parry by Horsham Meeting in 1807.*

Next steps to consider:

1. To continue researching the records of this family, we would move backward and check for the marriage record for David and Elizabeth in the Horsham Monthly Meeting minutes. Below is an image from the index of the Horsham Monthly Meeting. It would appear from the quantity of page numbers that there are numerous entries in the minutes to review for David and Elizabeth Parry.

2. We would also conduct a search of the Abington Monthly Meeting minutes (not shown) for the arrival of Elizabeth Parry in 1807 in order to determine that we have the correct Elizabeth Parry. If it is the correct Elizabeth Parry, we would search the same minutes (not shown) for any activities by the Parry children, such as marriages, certificates requested, etc. If it is not the correct Elizabeth Parry, we would go back to the Horsham Monthly Meeting minutes to search other activities by women with that name.

To recap, here are our research steps on Ancestry.com thus far:

FIGURE 14-21: Index for Horsham Meeting records showing a list of page numbers where the names "David Parry" and "Elizabeth Parry" appear in the records.

1. We received a shaky leaf on our online tree on Ancestry.com and decided to focus our research on David Parry. We knew his approximate age, that his wife was Elizabeth, and that they lived in the Philadelphia area. We didn't know he was a Quaker and didn't know about their children—we wanted to find out their names.

2. We started with the *Hinshaw Index to Quaker Records, 1680–1940*, and found a card indicating that a David and Elizabeth Parry moved from one meeting to another in 1795.

3. We consulted the list of abbreviations on the home page of the *Hinshaw Index to Quaker Records, 1680–1940* to find out two things: one was the meeting name located in the upper left corner. The other was the abbreviations used on the card. We could read the name of the meeting where they came from: Horsham M.M.

4. Not knowing anything about the two meetings, we looked in the *U.S and Canada, Quaker Monthly Meetings Index, 1671–2010.* We entered the meeting names and found their locations.

5. We then charted the two meetings on a Google map and found that this family moved into the northern part of Philadelphia from about 17 miles north of town.

6. We found another card for this family in the *Hinshaw Index to Quaker Records, 1680–1940.* This card indicated that the family had two more children, and it appears (from using the abbreviation codes) that they were granted a certificate to move to Buckingham Monthly Meeting.

7. We again checked the *U.S. and Canada, Quaker Monthly Meetings Index, 1671–2010* to determine where Buckingham Monthly Meeting was located (Bucks County, PA); we then charted it on a Google map.

8. Buckingham Monthly Meeting was not one of the meetings included in the Hinshaw abstraction project, so there are no cards for it in his collection. We researched the original minutes of the meeting using the *U.S., Quaker Meeting Records, 1681–1994* database. The names in this database were keyed by Ancestry.com, which makes them searchable. We entered the terms "David Parry" and "Bucks County." We found an entry with a date very close to when the family left the Philadelphia Northern District Monthly Meeting. When we clicked on "View Record," we found an entry in the Women's Monthly Meeting minutes that suggested we had identified the correct family.

9. We continued looking for David Parry in the entries in the *U.S., Quaker Meeting Records, 1681–1994* database. Each one linked us directly to the original meeting records.

10. It appears that after only a few short years, David and Elizabeth moved back to Philadelphia

from Buckingham Monthly Meeting. They added a daughter, Mary (see Card #3). We don't know why the family kept moving—it could have been for employment, because they had family in multiple locations, or for some other reason.

11. Eight months after they settled in Philadelphia, David died (see Card # 4).

12. By reading through other cards in the *Hinshaw Index to Quaker Records, 1680–1940*, we discovered that Elizabeth had another child and intended to move back to Horsham.

Here are some points to consider if we were to dive deeper to find more answers:

1. We don't know Elizabeth's maiden name yet. To find her record of marriage to David, we would trace the couple backward from our starting point to find their records in the Horsham Monthly Meeting minutes. If they weren't married under the care of the Horsham Monthly Meeting, we would most likely find a record of their arrival from another meeting. Then we would research the records of that meeting to find their marriage record. By locating the marriage record, we could learn the names of their parents and to which meetings they belonged.

2. We don't know what happened to the children who went to the Abington Monthly Meeting. We would research in the *U.S., Quaker Meeting Records, 1681–1994* database to find them in the Abington Monthly Meeting minutes. Perhaps they stayed there, and we would find marriage records for them.

3. What if the *U.S., Quaker Meeting Records, 1681–1994* database doesn't have the books for the year we are interested in researching? This database contains records that were on film at Swarthmore, Haverford, Earlham, and Guilford colleges. There are records that were not converted to microfilm; those originals must be consulted at the repository where they are stored. To determine which record books exist, which are on film, and which are still in paper form, go to the *U.S. and Canada, Quaker Monthly Meeting Historical Data, 1671–2010*. This database contains the information found on QuakerMeetings.com. Enter the name of the meeting; select the correct meeting from the list of meetings with similar names (there is usually more than one meeting with the same name); and click on it. You will see which records are known to exist, which have been filmed, and where they reside.

For example, if you were researching the records of the Horsham Monthly Meeting, you would want to use the "Browse" function (on the right-hand side of the page) in the *U.S., Quaker Meeting Records, 1681–1994* database on Ancestry.com.

> Select "Pennsylvania."
> Then select "Montgomery" County.
> Then select "Horsham Monthly Meeting."

There will be a drop-down menu of all the titles that were filmed from that meeting and that appear on Ancestry.com. Compare that list to the "Records Known Extant" list in the *U.S. and Canada, Quaker Monthly Meeting Historical Data, 1671–2010* database. (See figure below.)

Consult: **"Records Known Extant":** This indicates that Swarthmore has the original minute books, which are from the years listed.

Consult: **"Where Records are Kept":** This tells us three things: Swarthmore has the original books; there is microfilm at Haverford; and there is microfilm at the Family History Library in Salt Lake City.

Records Known Extant:	Swarthmore: Minutes 1782-1954, Women Minutes 1782-1793, 1819-1885, Marriages 1782-1953, Removals 1783-1940, Births 1713-1901, Deaths 1768-1889, Memb 1713-1947, Memb Transfers 1880-1940, Burials 1718-1968, M and E 1786-1944
Where Records are Kept:	Swarthmore Mf Haverford. Lds 20400, -16, -63, 383525

FIGURE 14-22: an enlargement of a portion of 14-23

North America, Quaker Monthly Meetings Index, 1671-2010	
Meeting Name:	Horsham
Latest Yearly Meeting:	Philadelphia Yearly Meeting
State or Province:	Pennsylvania
County:	Montgomery
Physical Location:	Horsham 19044, Meetinghouse Rd. and S.R. 611
Website:	View Website
Records Known Extant:	Swarthmore: Minutes 1782-1954, Women Minutes 1782-1793, 1819-1885, Marriages 1782-1953, Removals 1783-1940, Births 1713-1901, Deaths 1768-1889, Memb 1713-1947, Memb Transfers 1880-1940, Burials 1718-1968, M and E 1786-1944
Where Records are Kept:	Swarthmore Mf Haverford. Lds 20400, -16, -63, 383525
Comments:	Bound James E Hazard Complete-Name Genealogical Abstracts At Friends Historical Library, Swarthmore, Pa
Date Granted:	05 Aug 1782
Date of First Meeting:	29 Aug 1782
Date Laid Down:	Active
Branches:	Hicksite 29 Aug 1827 - 1955 Merger
Affiliations:	Philadelphia Quarterly Meeting Until 06 Feb 1786; Abington Quarterly Meeting After 04 May 1786
Subordinates:	Byberry Pm Until 1810Upper Dublin Pm 1816-1941Warminster Pm 1841-1953
Before and After:	Pm 1717-1959 From Abington Monthly Meeting
Records Website:	View Website
Preparative Record:	View Website

FIGURE 14-23: Meeting Name: Horshsam. Ancestry.com. U.S. and Canada, Quaker Monthly Meeting Historical Data, 1671-2010. Original data: Hill, Thomas C., Monthly Meetings in North America: A Quaker Index. Earlham College, Richmond, Indiana.

If you are interested in viewing any LDS film, such as those listed for Horsham Meeting in the example above, you can arrange to have it sent to your local LDS Family History Center. Use the film number listed under "Where Records are Kept" to order them. As you can see from the example, the film numbers for Horsham are *LDS 20400, 20416, 20463, and 383252.*

Check FamilySearch.org for the location of the closest LDS Family History Center to your home.

I hope that by reading through this case study, you are more familiar with some of the Quaker Collections appearing on Ancestry.com. Having even a portion of the Quaker Meeting records online is a great boon to Quaker research. It does take some repetition to get comfortable with using the abbreviations in the Hinshaw Index, but you will soon be reading through them with ease. Don't give up, your Quaker ancestors want to be found!

Appendix A
Hinshaw Unpublished Index Code List

Meeting Name	Meeting Code	State
Casa Grand Valley Monthly Meeting	CGC	Arizona
Alamitos Monthly Meeting	AC	California
Earlham Monthly Meeting	EC	California
East Whittier Monthly Meeting	EWC	California
Lindsay Monthly Meeting	LC	California
Oakland Monthly Meeting	OC	California
Owengo Monthly Meeting	OWC	California
Ramona Monthly Meeting	RC	California
San Jose Monthly Meeting	SJP	California
South Los Angeles Monthly Meeting	SLC	California
Stony Ford Monthly Meeting	SFC	California
Whittier Monthly Meeting	WMM Cal	California
Wildomar Monthly Meeting	WC	California
Colorado Springs Monthly Meeting	CSN	Colorado
La Junta Heights Monthly Meeting	LJN	Colorado
Mount Carmel Monthly Meeting	MCN	Colorado
Boise Monthly Meeting	BN	Idaho
Melba Monthly Meeting	MN	Idaho
Star Monthly Meeting	SN	Idaho
Ash Grove Monthly Meeting	AG	Illinois
Blue Island Monthly Meeting	BI	Illinois
Chicago Monthly Meeting (Hicksite)	CH (H)	Illinois
Chicago Monthly Meeting (Orthodox)	CH (O)	Illinois
Chicago Monthly Meeting (West Side)	CH	Illinois
Clear Creek Monthly Meeting	CCMM-PCI	Illinois
East Jordan Monthly Meeting	EJ	Illinois

Meeting Name	Meeting Code	State
Elwood Monthly Meeting	E	Illinois
Georgetown Monthly Meeting	GTMM-VCI	Illinois
Hyde Park (Chicago, Ill) Monthly Meeting	57 ILL	Illinois
Onarga Monthly Meeting	O ILL	Illinois
Plainfield Monthly Meeting	PFMM-ILL	Illinois
Richland Monthly Meeting	R ILL	Illinois
Ridge Farm Monthly Meeting	RFMM	Illinois
Vermillion Monthly Meeting	VMM	Illinois
Watseka Monthly Meeting (Orthodox)	W ILL	Illinois
Amboy Monthly Meeting	PCAMM	Indiana
Amo Monthly Meeting	AMM-HCI	Indiana
Anderson Monthly Meeting	A-IND	Indiana
Arba Monthly Meeting	AMM-RCI	Indiana
Back Creek Monthly Meeting	BCMM-GCI	Indiana
Barbers Mill Monthly Meeting	B-IND	Indiana
Beech Grove Monthly Meeting	BG-IND	Indiana
Beech Grove Monthly Meeting (Conservative)	BGINDC	Indiana
Bloomingdale Monthly Meeting	BFMM-PCI	Indiana
Blue River Monthly Meeting	BRMM-WCI	Indiana
Bridgeport Monthly Meeting	BR-IND	Indiana
Camden Monthly Meeting (Hicksite)	CMM-IND	Indiana
Carmel Monthly Meeting	RLMM-HCI	Indiana
Centerville or West Grove Monthly Meeting	WGMM-WCI	Indiana
Cherry Grove Monthly Meeting	CGMM-RCI	Indiana
Chester Monthly Meeting	CMM-WCI	Indiana
Coloma Monthly Meeting	C-IND	Indiana
Deer Creek Monthly Meeting	DCMM-GCI	Indiana
Deer Creek Monthly Meeting of Anti-Slavery Friends	DCMMASF-GCI	Indiana
Dublin Monthly Meeting	MM-WCI	Indiana
Duck Creek Monthly Meeting	DCMM-HCI	Indiana
East Branch Monthly Meeting	EB-IND	Indiana
Fairfield Monthly Meeting	FFMM-HCI	Indiana
Fairmount Monthly Meeting	FMMM-GCI	Indiana
Fall Creek Monthly Meeting	FCMM-MCI	Indiana
Farmer's Institute Monthly Meeting	GFMM-TCI	Indiana

Meeting Name	Meeting Code	State
Farmland Monthly Meeting	FLMM-RCI	Indiana
Fountain City Monthly Meeting	FCMM-WCI	Indiana
Greentown Monthly Meeting	G-IND	Indiana
Greenwood Monthly Meeting	GR-IND	Indiana
Hazel Dell Monthly Meeting	H-IND	Indiana
Hemlock Monthly Meeting	HE-IND	Indiana
Hinkles Creek Monthly Meeting	HCMM-HCI	Indiana
Honey Creek Monthly Meeting	HCMM-VCI	Indiana
Hopewell Monthly Meeting (Vermillion Co, Ind)	HWMM-HCI	Indiana
Indianapolis Monthly Meeting	I-IND	Indiana
Jonesboro Monthly Meeting	JBMM-GCI	Indiana
Knightstown Monthly Meeting (form. Raysville MM)	RVMM-HCI	Indiana
Kokomo Monthly Meeting	K-IND	Indiana
La Porte Monthly Meeting	LP-IND	Indiana
Lamong Monthly Meeting (form. Union Grove MM)	L-IND	Indiana
Lapel Monthly Meeting	LA-IND	Indiana
Maple Grove Monthly Meeting	MG-IND	Indiana
Marion Monthly Meeting (form. Mississinewa MM)	MMM-GCI	Indiana
Marshall Monthly Meeting (form. Poplar Grove MM)	M-IND	Indiana
Mill Creek Monthly Meeting	MCMM-HCI	Indiana
Milo Monthly Meeting	MI-IND	Indiana
Muncie Monthly Meeting	MMM-DCI	Indiana
New Hope Monthly Meeting	NH-IND	Indiana
New London Monthly Meeting (form. Honey Creek MM)	HCMM-HCI-NL	Indiana
New Salem Monthly Meeting	NS-IND	Indiana
New White River Monthly Meeting	NWRMM-RCI	Indiana
Noblesville Monthly Meeting	N-IND	Indiana
Oak Ridge Monthly Meeting	ORMM-GCI	Indiana
Paoli Monthly Meeting (form. Lick Creek MM)	LCMM-OCI	Indiana
Paoli Monthly Meeting	PMM-OCI	Indiana
Plainfield Monthly Meeting	PL-IND	Indiana
Plainfield Monthly Meeting (Conservative)	PL-IND-C	Indiana
Pleasant Hill Monthly Meeting	PH-IND	Indiana
Pleasant Plain Monthly Meeting	PP-IND	Indiana
Poplar Ridge Monthly Meeting	PR-IND	Indiana

Meeting Name	Meeting Code	State
Poplar Run Monthly Meeting	PRMM-RCI	Indiana
Portland Monthly Meeting	PMM-JCI	Indiana
Providence Monthly Meeting	P-IND	Indiana
Rush Creek Monthly Meeting	R-IND	Indiana
Salem Monthly Meeting	SCSMM-UCI	Indiana
Sand Creek Monthly Meeting (form. Driftwood MM)	DWMM-BCI	Indiana
Sheridan Monthly Meeting	S-IND	Indiana
Shiloh Monthly Meeting	SH-IND	Indiana
South Marion Monthly Meeting	SMMM-GCI	Indiana
South Wabash Monthly Meeting	SWMM-WCI	Indiana
Spiceland Monthly Meeting	SLMM-HCI	Indiana
Sugar Plain Monthly Meeting	SPMM-BCI	Indiana
Sugar River Monthly Meeting	SRMM-MCI	Indiana
Union Monthly Meeting	U-IND	Indiana
Wabash Monthly Meeting	WMM-WCI	Indiana
Walnut Ridge Monthly Meeting	WRMM-RCI	Indiana
West Indianapolis Monthly Meeting	WI-IND	Indiana
West Richmond Monthly Meeting	WRMM-WCI	Indiana
West Union Monthly Meeting	WUMM-MCI	Indiana
Westfield Monthly Meeting	WFMM-HCI	Indiana
Westfield Monthly Meeting (Conservative)	WFMM-HCIC	Indiana
White Lick Monthly Meeting	WLMM-MCI	Indiana
White River Monthly Meeting	WRMM-RCI	Indiana
White River Monthly Meeting (Conservative)	WRMM-RCI-C	Indiana
Williamsburg Monthly Meeting (form. Dover MM)	DMM-WCI	Indiana
Winchester Monthly Meeting	WMM-RCI	Indiana
Ackworth Monthly Meeting	TRI	Iowa
Albia Monthly Meeting	AI	Iowa
Albion Monthly Meeting	ALI	Iowa
Arnolds Park Monthly Meeting	API	Iowa
Bangor Monthly Meeting	BI	Iowa
Bear Creek Monthly Meeting	BCI	Iowa
Bear Creek Monthly Meeting (Conservative)	BCIC	Iowa
Bloomfield Monthly Meeting	BLI	Iowa
Bloomington Monthly Meeting	BLOI	Iowa

Meeting Name	Meeting Code	State
Buffalo Monthly Meeting	BUI	Iowa
Burr Oaks Monthly Meeting	BOI	Iowa
Canby Monthly Meeting	CAI	Iowa
Casey Monthly Meeting	CASI	Iowa
Cedar Creek Monthly Meeting	CCI	Iowa
Center Monthly Meeting	CEI	Iowa
Chester Monthly Meeting	CI	Iowa
Chestnut Hill Monthly Meeting	CHI	Iowa
Clay Center Preparative Meeting	CLCI	Iowa
Coal Creek Monthly Meeting (Conservative)	COCIC	Iowa
Des Moines Monthly Meeting	DMI	Iowa
Earlham Monthly Meeting	EAI	Iowa
Fairview Monthly Meeting	FAI	Iowa
Greenville Monthly Meeting	GRI	Iowa
Grinnell Monthly Meeting	GI	Iowa
Hamilton Monthly Meeting	HII	Iowa
Hartland Monthly Meeting	HAI	Iowa
Hickory Grove Monthly Meeting	HGI	Iowa
Hickory Grove Monthly Meeting (Conservative)	HGIC	Iowa
Hiteman Monthly Meeting	HITI	Iowa
Honey Creek Monthly Meeting	HCI	Iowa
Hopewell Rubio Monthly Meeting	HRI	Iowa
Hubbard Monthly Meeting	HUI	Iowa
Hynes Monthly Meeting	HYI	Iowa
Ida Grove Monthly Meeting	IGI	Iowa
Illinois Grove Monthly Meeting	ILIG	Iowa
Indianapolis Monthly Meeting	INI	Iowa
Iowa Falls Monthly Meeting	IOI	Iowa
Le Grande Monthly Meeting	LGI	Iowa
Liberty Center Monthly Meeting	LCI	Iowa
Liberty Monthly Meeting	LI	Iowa
Linden Monthly Meeting	LII	Iowa
Lynnville Monthly Meeting	LYI	Iowa
Marietta Monthly Meeting	MII	Iowa
Marshalltown Monthly Meeting	MAI	Iowa

Meeting Name	Meeting Code	State
Middle River Monthly Meeting	MRI	Iowa
Motor Monthly Meeting	MOI	Iowa
Muscatine Monthly Meeting	MUI	Iowa
New Sharon Monthly Meeting	NSI	Iowa
North Branch Monthly Meeting	NBIC	Iowa
North H Street Monthly Meeting	NHI	Iowa
Oak Grove Monthly Meeting	OGI	Iowa
Oak Run Monthly Meeting	ORI	Iowa
Oskaloosa City Monthly Meeting	OSCI	Iowa
Oskaloosa Monthly Meeting	OSI	Iowa
Paton Monthly Meeting	PI	Iowa
Paullina Monthly Meeting	PAIC	Iowa
Pilot Grove Monthly Meeting	PGI	Iowa
Pilot Grove Monthly Meeting (Conservative)	PGIC	Iowa
Pleasant Chapel Monthly Meeting	PCI	Iowa
Pleasant Plain Monthly Meeting	PPI	Iowa
Pleasant Ridge Monthly Meeting	PRI	Iowa
Richland Monthly Meeting	RI	Iowa
Rosemount Monthly Meeting	ROI	Iowa
Salem Monthly Meeting	SAI	Iowa
Salem Monthly Meeting (Conservative)	SAIC	Iowa
Scranton Monthly Meeting	SCRI	Iowa
Searsboro Monthly Meeting	SEI	Iowa
Sheldon Monthly Meeting	SHI	Iowa
Smyrna Monthly Meeting	SMI	Iowa
Spencer Monthly Meeting	SPI	Iowa
Springdale Monthly Meeting	SPRI	Iowa
Springville Monthly Meeting	SIC	Iowa
Stanford Monthly Meeting	STAI	Iowa
Stavanger Monthly Meeting (Conservative)	STVIC	Iowa
Stockport Monthly Meeting	STOI	Iowa
Stuart Monthly Meeting	SGI	Iowa
Sugar Creek Monthly Meeting	SCI	Iowa
Summit Grove Monthly Meeting (Conservative)	SGIC	Iowa
Walnut Center Monthly Meeting	WCI	Iowa

Meeting Name	Meeting Code	State
Wapsinonoc Monthly Meeting	WAI	Iowa
West Branch Monthly Meeting	WBI	Iowa
West Branch Monthly Meeting (Conservative)	WBIC	Iowa
Willow Creek Preparative Meeting	WCRI	Iowa
Winneshick Monthly Meeting	WI	Iowa
Wright Monthly Meeting	WRI	Iowa
Fowler Monthly Meeting	FOK	Kansas
Friendship Monthly Meeting	FK	Kansas
Greencastle Monthly Meeting	GK	Kansas
Harmony Monthly Meeting	HAK	Kansas
Harveyville Monthly Meeting	HYK	Kansas
Haviland Monthly Meeting	HK	Kansas
Hopewell Monthly Meeting	HOK	Kansas
Independence Monthly Meeting	IK	Kansas
La Harpe Monthly Meeting	LHK	Kansas
Liberal Monthly Meeting	LK	Kansas
Lone Star Monthly Meeting	LSK	Kansas
Millcreek Monthly Meeting	MK	Kansas
Mount Ayr Monthly Meeting	MAK	Kansas
Mount Tabor Monthly Meeting	MTK	Kansas
North Branch Monthly Meeting	NBK	Kansas
Paradise Monthly Meeting	PK	Kansas
Pleasant Plain Monthly Meeting	PPK	Kansas
Pleasant Ridge Monthly Meeting	PRK	Kansas
Pleasant Valley Monthly Meeting	PVK	Kansas
Prairie Center Monthly Meeting	PCK	Kansas
Ramona Monthly Meeting	RK	Kansas
Rock Creek Monthly Meeting	RCK	Kansas
Rose Valley Monthly Meeting	RVK	Kansas
Saint Charles Monthly Meeting	SCK	Kansas
Seiling Monthly Meeting	SK	Kansas
Springdale Monthly Meeting	SPK	Kansas
Stafford Monthly Meeting	STK	Kansas
Stanwood Monthly Meeting	SWK	Kansas
Sterling Monthly Meeting	SLK	Kansas

Meeting Name	Meeting Code	State
Timbered Hills Monthly Meeting	THK	Kansas
Toledo Monthly Meeting	TK	Kansas
Tonganoxie Monthly Meeting	TOL	Kansas
Trego Center Monthly Meeting	TRK	Kansas
University Monthly Meeting	UK	Kansas
Walnut Creek Monthly Meeting	WCK	Kansas
West Glendale Monthly Meeting	WGK	Kansas
Wichita Monthly Meeting	WIK	Kansas
Birch Lake Monthly Meeting	BLMM-CCM	Michigan
Detroit Monthly Meeting	D-Mich	Michigan
Long Lake Monthly Meeting	L-Mich	Michigan
Onaway Monthly Meeting	O-Mich	Michigan
Traverse City Monthly Meeting	T-Mich	Michigan
Vandalia Monthly Meeting	V-Mich	Michigan
Highland Monthly Meeting	HII	Minnesota
Minneapolis Monthly Meeting	MII	Minnesota
Union Monthly Meeting	UI	Minnesota
Fairview Monthly Meeting	FAK	Missouri
Kansas City Monthly Meeting	KCK	Missouri
Union Monthly Meeting	UNK	Missouri
Central City Monthly Meeting	CCN	Nebraska
Community Friends Monthly Meeting	CON	Nebraska
Elk Valley Monthly Meeting	EN	Nebraska
Friendsdale Monthly Meeting	FN	Nebraska
Lincoln Executive Monthly Meeting (Hicksite)	LN	Nebraska
North Loup Monthly Meeting	NLN	Nebraska
Plainview Monthly Meeting	PN	Nebraska
Platte Valley Monthly Meeting	PLN	Nebraska
Pleasant Hill Monthly Meeting	PHN	Nebraska
Spring Bank Monthly Meeting	SBN	Nebraska
Evesham Monthly Meeting	EVP	New Jersey
Haddonfield Monthly Meeting	HP	New Jersey
Mount Holly Monthly Meeting	MHP	New Jersey
Woodbury Monthly Meeting	WPH	New Jersey
Cherokee Monthly Meeting	CHK	Oklahoma

Meeting Name	Meeting Code	State
New Hope Monthly Meeting	NHK	Oklahoma
Siloam Monthly Meeting	SIK	Oklahoma
Vera Monthly Meeting	VK	Oklahoma
Wyandotte Monthly Meeting (form. Grand River MM)	GRK	Oklahoma
Chester Monthly Meeting	CMCCP	Pennsylvania
Chester Monthly Meeting	CMM:CCP	Pennsylvania
Chester Monthly Meeting (Hicksite)	CMM:CCPH	Pennsylvania
Concord Monthly Meeting	ConMM	Pennsylvania
Darby Monthly Meeting	DMM-DCP	Pennsylvania
Darby Monthly Meeting (Orthodox)	O DMM-DCP	Pennsylvania
Exeter Monthly Meeting	EXP	Pennsylvania
Frankford Monthly Meeting	FP	Pennsylvania
Goshen Monthly Meeting	GOP	Pennsylvania
Gwynedd Monthly Meeting	GWP	Pennsylvania
Kennett Monthly Meeting	KP	Pennsylvania
London Grove Monthly Meeting	LGP	Pennsylvania
Muncy-Millville Monthly Meeting	JEE	Pennsylvania
New Garden Monthly Meeting	NGPA	Pennsylvania
Philadelphia Northern District Monthly Meeting	PNDP	Pennsylvania
Philadelphia Southern District Monthly Meeting	PSDP	Pennsylvania
Stroudsburgh Monthly Meeting	SP	Pennsylvania
Aurora Monthly Meeting	AUI	South Dakota
Harmony Monthly Meeting	HARI	South Dakota
Lyman County Monthly Meeting	LCOI	South Dakota
Mount Vernon Monthly Meeting	MVI	South Dakota
Kedron Monthly Meeting	KI	Wisconsin
Sturgeon Bay Monthly Meeting	STBI	Wisconsin
Valton Monthly Meeting	VI	Wisconsin

Appendix B

Quaker Biographical Sketches

BIOGRAPHICAL RESOURCES ABOUT THE VERY early Quakers are not plentiful for those members whose names are less well-known. This collection of 563 biographical sketches ranges in date from 1682-1800, and will be most useful for those who are researching members of the Philadelphia Yearly Meeting. The original title is: Quaker Biographical Sketches of Ministers and Elders, and other concerned members of the Yearly Meeting of Philadelphia, [1682-1800], edited by Willard Heiss, 1972.

The entries were compiled by Quaker historian Willard Heiss, from a series of biographies published in The Friend (Philadelphia) from 1853 to 1863. Mr. Heiss retained references to people and places but removed "extensive passages of pious admonitions and religious exhortations". This index includes the volume and page number from the original magazine publication as well as the page number from Heiss' book. Remember that the spelling of names changed over time; it is wise to check out names that are even reasonably close to those of your ancestors. An online copy of Quaker Biographical Sketches can be found at FamilySearch.org/catalog. Check worldcat.org to find a hard copy of the book in a library near you.

Name	Friend Vol. - Page	Heiss Book Page Number
Abbott, Samuel	33-45	226
Allen, Jedidiah	28 269	68
Anderson, Margaret	35-140	304
Andrews, Benajah	33-148	237
Andrews, Peter	31-268	201
Andrews, Samuel	29-20	92
Andrews, Samuel & Mary	28-166	59

Name	Friend Vol. - Page	Heiss Book Page Number
Antrim, Isaac	30-212	155
Armitt, John	33-84	230
Armitt, Sophia	29-413	132
Ashbridge, Elizabeth	31-212	193
Ashton, Mary	33-12	222
Atkinson, Thomas	27-172	11
Atkinson, William	31-76	169
Austin, John	28-60	51

APPENDIX B: Quaker Biographical Sketches

Name	Friend Vol. - Page	Heiss Book Page Number	Name	Friend Vol. - Page	Heiss Book Page Number
Austin, Nicholas	35-116	302	Bunting, Alice	31-268	200
Bacon, John	31-164	185	Bunting, Mary	35-75	297
Bailey, Olive	33-324	250	Bunting, Samuel	28-396	88
Baldwin, John	30-244	161	Burr, Joseph	33-340	252
Baldwin, William	28-348	80	Busby, Richard	30-261	162
Ball, Catharine	33-141	235	Butcher, Margaret	32-388	217
Barrow, Robert	27-364	41	Buzby, Thomas	35-276	315
Barton, Edward	29-396	129	Cadwallader, John	30-101	147
Bennett, Rebecca	32-340	213	Cadwallader, Mary	29-268	111
Bevan, Barbara	28-45	50	Cadwallader, Morgan	27-373	42
Bevan, Eleanor	30-212	155	Caldwell, Betty	32-323	213
Biles, Jane	28-93	53	Caldwell, Vincent	28-339	79
Biles, William	28-109	54	Carleton, Hannah	32-388	217
Blackburn, Christopher	28-380	84	Carnby, Thomas	30-92	145
Blakely, William	29-396	129	Carpenter, Hannah	29-260	110
Blunstone, John	28-396	87	Cathrall, Rachel	35-276	315
Blunstone, Phebe	31-61	167	Chalkley, Martha	28-157	58
Bolton, Elizabeth	28-60	50	Champion, Esther	28-190	62
Bolton, Margaret	30-13	135	Champion, Matthew	29-374	126
Bond, John	30-261	163	Chapman, Abraham	31-164	185
Boone, Deborah	32-403	220	Chapman, Joseph	31-124	179
Booth, Joseph	29-340	120	Child, Cephas	31-268	201
Borton, Obadiah	33-53	226	Child, Isaac	35-84	299
Bradshaw, Thomas	29-244	108	Churchman, John	36-36	320
Brasey, Thomas	27-213	19	Churchman, Margaret	35-132	303
Breintnall, Jane	29- 21	93	Clare, Esther	30-36	138
Bringhurst, John	31-108	176	Claypoole, James	27-172	12
Brinton, Ann	33-76	229	Clough, George	29-316	117a
Brown, James	35-212	307	Coate, Marmaduke	29-276	111
Brown, John	32-307	212	Coates, Beulah	30-13	134
Brown, Joshua	34-36	266	Coggeshall, Martha	29-365	124
Brown, Preserve	33-20	222	Coleston, William	29-268	111
Brown, Thomas	32-301	211	Collier, John	29-252	109
Bryan, Rebecca	30-276	165	Comfort, Stephen	35-236	309

Name	Friend Vol. - Page	Heiss Book Page Number	Name	Friend Vol. - Page	Heiss Book Page Number
Conrad, Cornelius	35-132	303	Duell, Thomas	31-268	201
Conrad, Dennis	29-268	111	Dunkan, William	28-197	63
Cooper, Esther	28-51	50	Dunkin, John	29-268	111
Cooper, Hannah	31-148	182	Dunn, Deborah	35-212	307
Cooper, John	29-316	117	Dunn, Zaccheus	35-268	313
Cooper, Joseph	31-61	168	Durborough, Elizabeth	28-380	84
Cooper, Sybil	32-413	220	Durborough, Hugh	30-5	132
Cooper, William	28-142	57	Dyer, John	29-405	131
Coppock, Aaron	29-68	96	Eckley, John	27-205	17
Corlies, Deborah	32-340	213	Edwards, William	33-148	236
Cowperthwaite, Elizabeth	27-364	42	Elfreth, Jeremiah	35-251	312
Cramer, Andrew	30-244	161	Elgar, Joseph	29-365	124
Crips, Nathaniel	30-229	158	Ellis, Hugh	33-132	234
Croasdale, Ezra	30-6	133	Ellis, Jane	35-228	309
Croasdale, Grace	35-100	301	Ellis, Margaret	29-331	119
Cumming, Thomas	33-337	251	Ellis, Margaret	33-293	246
Daniel, Elizabeth	33-28	224	Ellis, Rowland	29-316	117a
Daniel, James	29-140	101	Ellis, Sage	33-46	226
Davenport, Sarah	28-405	88	Ellis, Thomas	27-179	13
Daves, Isaac	31-108	176	Ellis, Thomas	33-20	223
Daves, Priscilla	35-228	308	Ely, Hugh	35-189	307
David, Elinor	29-374	126	Ely, Phebe	35-284	316
David, Lewis	30-20	135	England, Joseph	31-44	165
Davis, David	31-148	182	Estaugh, Elizabeth	33-68	229
Davis, John	31-61	167	Estaugh, John	30-108	148
Davis, Rebecca	35-251	311	Evans, Cadwallader	30-220	157
Dawes, David	31-53	166	Evans, Elizabeth	30-276	165
Deacon, George	29-20	92	Evans, Ellen	33-164	238
Dean, Lydia	31-117	177	Evans, Evan	30-252	162
Delaval, John	27-276	30	Evans, Hannah	30-252	162
Denn, John	29-357	123	Evans, John	28-60	51
Dillwyn, John	31-44	165	Evans, John	31-284	203
Dilworth, James	27-398	44	Evans, Lowry	33-102	231
Duckett, Thomas	27-405	45	Evans, Mary	35-91	300

APPENDIX B: Quaker Biographical Sketches

Name	Friend Vol. - Page	Heiss Book Page Number
Evans, Owen	32-301	211
Evans, Rebecca	35-284	315
Evans, Robert	29-396	130
Evans, William	29-260	111
Everden, Thomas	28-109	54
Farmer, John	28-310	75
Farrington, Abraham	32-340	214
Fawcett, Walter	28-339	78
Fearn, Josiah	29-316	117a
Fearson, Peter	33-108	232
F e l l, Benjamin	32-397	219
F e l l, Joseph	30-20	135
F i e l d, Mary	33-300	247
Fisher, John	33-156	237
Fletcher, Elizabeth	31-44	166
Fletcher, Robert	29-68	97
Fletcher, Robert	29-374	126
Forrest, Joan	29-348	121
Foster, Josiah	35-116	302
Foulke, Ann	35-278	314
Foulke, Cadwallader	30-204	155
Foulke, Gwinn	33-37	225
Foulke, Hugh	33-12	222
Foulke, Thomas	33-101	231
Foulke, William	36-59	320
French, Richard	30-229	158
French, Robert	33-28	224
Gardiner, Thomas	27-340	39
Garretson, Remembrance	28-197	63
Garrett, Jane	29-38	126
Garwood, Mary	33-116	233
George, Richard	35-189	307
Gilbert, Joseph	33-196	239
Gill, Robert	27-380	43

Name	Friend Vol. - Page	Heiss Book Page Number
Glaister, Joseph	28-331	77
Goodson, John	29-252	109
Goodson, Thomas	36-36	319
Gove, Richard	28-125	55
Grave, Samuel	30-30	135
Gray, George	28-276	69
Gray, Naomi	28-93	52
Greave, Jonathan	35-309	317
Griffith, Abraham	33-29	224
Griffith, Alice	31-53	166
Griffith, Thomas & Elizabeth	29-236	107
Haig, William & Mary	28-325	77
Haines, Esther	28-339	79
Haines, John	29-268	111
Hales, Susanna	31-132	180
Hammons, Lydia	31-124	179
Hammons, William	31-164	185
Hampton, Joseph	33-340	252
Hancock, Richard	29-365	123
Harker, Grace	30-268	164
Harper, Eliaphal	30-261	163
Harrison, James	27-157	9
Harvey, Elizabeth	31-164	185
Harvey, John	31-148	182
Harvey, Martha	30-220	157
Harvey, Peter	35-189	306
Haydock, Elizabeth	33-116	233
Hayes, Elizabeth	30-20	136
Hayhurst, Cuthbert	27-116	1
Hearn, Sarah	29-252	108
Heritage, Joseph	31-284	203
Heston, Jacob	33-300	247
Hill, Hannah	29-236	106

Name	Friend Vol. - Page	Heiss Book Page Number
Hingston, Abel	30-268	163
Hodgkins, Millicent	27-243	24
Holcombe, Jacob	31-44	160
Hollingshead, John	31-53	162
Hollingshead, Mary	33-116	233
Hollingsworth, Isaac	33-4	221
Hollingsworth, Thomas	31-132	180
Holton, Elizabeth	32-301	211
Homer, John	28-405	88
Horne, William	35-251	312
Hoskins, Jane	33-204	240
Hoskins, Richard	28-6	46
Howell, Jacob	35-75	297
Hudson, William	30-181	151
Hugh, Jane	33-317	249
Hugh, Robert	28-6	47
Hughes, Aaron	31-132	180
Humphrey, Benjamin	29-404	130
Humphrey, John	29-404	131
Humphrey, Mary	33-293	246
Humphreys, Hannah	31-117	176
Hurford, Hannah	33-124	234
Ireland, Ruth	32-340	213
Jackson, Elizabeth	28-36	49
Jackson, Ralph	29-68	96
Jacobs, Mary	29-285	114
James, Aaron	31-124	179
James, Dinah	33-300	247
Janney, Elizabeth	35-140	304
Janney, Mary	33-340	252
Janney, Thomas	27-340	39
Jenkins, Abigail	31-117	177
Jennings, Samuel	28-70	51
Jerman, Margaret	30-13	134

Name	Friend Vol. - Page	Heiss Book Page Number
Jerman, Thomas	30-13	134
Jess, Zachary	28-396	87
John, Samuel	33-324	250
Johns, Richard	34-412	261
Jones, Arthur	30-36	138
Jones, Benjamin	30-276	165
Jones, Cadwallader	32-403	219
Jones, David	29-28	93
Jones, Edwards	29-396	129
Jones, Hannah	29-404	130
Jones, Jane	32-388	218
Jones, John	35-310	318
Jones, Margaret	30-181	151
Jones, Mary	29-76	97
Jones, Richard	35-140	304
Jones, Robert	35-268	313
Jones, Ruth	33-204	239
Jones, Thomas	29-252	109
Jordon, Benjamin	34-4	263
Jordon, Joseph	34-12	263
Jordon, Robert	30-45	139
Jordon, Robert, 1st	34-4	262
Jordon, Thomas & Margaret	34-4	262
Kenerdine, Richard	29-357	123
King, Joseph	33-54	227
Kinsey, Edmund	33-12	221
Kinsey, John	31-301	204
Kinsey, John, 2nd	31-84	170
Kinsey, John, 3rd	31-92	172
Kinsman, Hannah	28-339	79
Kirkbride, Joseph	29-.396	129
Kirkbride, Sarah	28-45	50
Knight, Mary	35-75	298

Name	Friend Vol. - Page	Heiss Book Page Number	Name	Friend Vol. - Page	Heiss Book Page Number
Knowles, Sarah	29-380	126	Lloyd, Thomas	33-365	254
Lancaster, Thomas	31-124	178	Longworth, Roger	27-148	7
Langhorn, Thomas	27-172	11	Lord, James	29-244	108
Large, Dorothy	32-301	211	Lord, Joshua	33-45	225
Large, Ebenezer	33-36	224	Lovett, Mary	32-388	217
Large, Robert	35-284	316	Lowden, John	28-181	61
Large, Samuel	33-181	238	Lucas, Edward	30-5	132
Lawrence, Ellen	31-76	169	Lucas, John	31-44	166
Lawrence, Henry	33-308	248	Lunday, Richard	35-212	307
Lawrence, William	29-357	123	Lynam, John & Margaret	27-364	42
Lawrie, William	35-284	316	M'Vaugh, Sarah	29-404	130
Lay, Sarah	29-380	126	Marriott, Mary	30-268	164
Laycock, John	31-117	177	Marshall, Abraham	33-344	253
Lee, Anthony	33-116	233	Marshall, Mary	35-100	301
Lee, John	29-148	102	Martyn, James	27-220	19
Levis, Elizabeth	35-332	318	Mather, Elizabeth	29-285	114
Levis, William	30-245	161	Mendenhall, Benjamin	30-6	133
Lewis, Ellis	31-76	170	Mendenhall, Benjamin, 2nd	30-196	153
Lewis, George	31-148	179	Mendenhall, Joseph	30-276	165
Lewis, Richard	29-252	109	Mendenhall, Moses	29-339	120
Lightfoot, Michael	31-148	182	Merideth, David	29-148	103
Lightfoot, Thomas	29-28	93	Middleton, Elizabeth	35-132	303
Lippincott, Elizabeth	29-143	132	Middleton, George	35-132	303
Lippincott, John	31-44	166	Middleton, John	33-156	237
Lippincott, Margaret	2-268	111	Milhouse, Sarah	36-30	320
Lippincott, Mary	35-140	304	Miller, Catharine	29-268	111
Lippincott, Remembrance	28-396	87	Miller, Margaret	33-156	237
Lippincott, Restore	30-20	135	Milner, Sarah	28-197	63
Lippincott, Richard	28-388	85	Mitchener, John	33-300	242
Livesey, Jonathan	33-148	237	Mitchener, Sarah	32-340	214
Lloyd, Deborah	30-20	136	Moore, Andrew	31-132	179
Lloyd, Evan	30-13	134	Moore, Ann	33-53	227
Lloyd, Grace	33-20	223	Moore, Mary	33-308	249
Lloyd, Thomas	27-300	34			

Name	Friend Vol. - Page	Heiss Book Page Number	Name	Friend Vol. - Page	Heiss Book Page Number
Morgan, Daniel	35-268	313	Pearson, Enoch	32-388	217
Morris, Anthony	28-356	81	Peirce, Ann	30-261	163
Morris, Anthony	29-20	92	Pemberton, Israel	31-141	181
Morris, Anthony	33-124	233	Pemberton, Rachel	33-156	237
Morris, Morris	33-148	236	Pennell, Mary	33-141	235
Morris, Phebe	35-84	299	Pencek, Elizabeth	31-268	201
Morris, Sarah	36-59	320	Penquite, Agnes	32-397	219
Morris, Susanna	31-173	186	Pharon, Jervis	31-293	204
Moss, Abraham	31-53	166	Phipps, Ann	30-212	155
Murfin, Sarah	33-92	230	Phipps, Sarah	29-68	97
Musgrave, Thomas	28-6	46	Pim, William	31-124	179
Nichols, Mary	35-116	302	Pleasants, John, 2nd	34-20	265
Nicholson, Abel	31-124	178	Pleasants, John & Jane	34-20	264
Nicholson, Elizabeth	32-404	220	Pleasants, Margaret	34-28	265
Nixon, William	30-268	164	Pleasants, Sarah	34-28	266
Norris, Mary	30-276	165	Pleasants, Thomas	34-20	265
Olive, Thomas	27-228	22	Potts, Joan	30-13	134
Orpwood, Edmund	29-252	109	Potts, Rachel	32-388	217
Osborn, Jane	29-285	114	Powell, Howell	29-339	120
Osborn, Richard	30-13	134	Powell, Samuel	31-268	201
Owen, Griffith	28-197	63	Preston, Margaret	30-20	136
Owen, Robert	27-364	41	Preston, Paul	29-348	122
Owen, Robert & Jane	27-124	2	Preston, Samuel	30-196	153
Owen, Sarah	29-357	123	Pugh, Ellis	28-284	71
Oxley, John	30-188	151	Pugh, Job	32-323	213
Palmer, David	29-339	120	Pugh, Phebe	31-268	201
Palmer, Jonathan	33-293	246	Pusey, Caleb	29-148	103
Parke, Thomas	29-413	131	Pusey, Joshua & Mary	33-21	223
Parker, Joseph	28-396	87	Radcliff, James	27-213	18
Parson, Ann	29-349	122	Raper Abigail	31-124	179
Paul, James	33-46	226	Raper, Caleb	30-229	158
Paxson, Abigail	30-268	164	Raper, Caleb	33-412	262
Paxson, William	29-365	123	Raper, Joshua	33-20	223
Peachy, William	27-198	16	Raper, Thomas & Abigail	33-412	261

APPENDIX B: Quaker Biographical Sketches

Name	Friend Vol. - Page	Heiss Book Page Number	Name	Friend Vol. - Page	Heiss Book Page Number
Redman, Thomas	33-324	250	Simcock, John	28-28	48
Reese, Edward	29-268	110	Simcock, John	35-268	313
Reese, Rebecca	29-357	123	Simcock, Mary	35-156	305
Ridgeway, Phebe	31-124	179	Skein, John	27-252	26
Ridgway, John	35-284	316	Slokam, Meribah	29-268	111
Ridgway, Thomas	28-396	88	Smedley, George	33-332	251
Roberts, Ann	31-101	174	Smith, Daniel	30-20	136
Roberts, Edward	35-75	297	Smith, Eleanor	28-60	51
Roberts, John	28-28	48	Smith, Elizabeth	30-252	161
Roberts, John	35-140	304	Smith, Elizabeth	35-236	310
Roberts, Mary	33-68	228	Smith, George	28-197	63
Roberts, Robert	35-68	296	Smith, Hannah	33-60	227
Roberts, Rowland	31-61	167	Smith, John	28-181	67
Robinson, George	29-404	130	Smith, John	33-332	251
Robinson, Katharine	30-244	160	Smith, John	35-156	305
Routledge, John	29-21	92	Smith, Mary	30-229	159
Routledge, Mary	29-148	103	Smith, Mary	31-293	204
Salkeld , John	33-372	255	Smith, Richard	31-124	178
Satterthwaite, Samuel	35-268	314	Smith, Richard, Jr	31-124	179
Scarborough, John	29-244	107	Smith, Richard, Jr	33-357	253
Scarborough, John	35-91	300	Somers, Edmund	30-212	155
Scarlett, John	35-212	308	Somers, Hannah	29-404	131
Scattergood, Thomas	30-212	156	Somers, John	28-396	87
Schooley, Samuel	33-45	226	Songhurst, John	27-188	15
Sharp, Judith	31-53	167	Sotcher, John	29-268	111
Sharpless, John	35-116	301	Southeby, William	28-293	73
Shinn, Thomas	31-125	179	Speakman, Mary	35-310	317
Shoemaker, Isaac	29-357	123	Speakman, Thomas	29-348	121
Shoemaker, Peter	30-13	134	Spicer, Samuel	29-292	114
Shotwell, Eleanor	33-92	231	Stackhouse, John	32-340	213
Shotwell, Elizabeth	32-404	220	Stacy, Mahlon	29-13	90
Shotwell, John	33-84	230	Stevens, Elizabeth	35-251	312
Shotwell, Mary	33-68	229	Stockdale, Jervis	29-68	97
Shotwell, Sarah	33-4	221	Stockdale, Phebe	29-404	131

Name	Friend Vol. - Page	Heiss Book Page Number
Stockdale, William	27-291	32
Sykes, Joanna	35-228	308
Sykes, John	35-189	306
Taylor, Christopher & Frances	27-124	3
Teague, Pentecost & Elizabeth	29-252	109
Test, Elizabeth	35-212	307
Thomas, Evan	30-244	160
Thomas, Evan	31-164	185
Thomas, John	27-117	1
Thomas, John	35-150	305
Thomas, Martha	29-148	103
Thomas, Samuel	31-212	193
Thomas, Thamer	35-140	304
Tilton, Amos	33-293	246
Tilton, John	29-316	117a
Tilton, Robert	33-102	232
Tilton, Thomas	33-116	233
Tomlinson, Joseph & Catherine	33-397	218
Townsend, Joseph	33-308	248
Townsend, Millicent	33-92	230
Townsend , Richard	29-380	127
Trotter, Benjamin	35-68	296
Trotter, William	31-76	170
Tyson, Priscilla	33-37	225
Tyson, Reiner	30-229	158
Tyson, Sarah	35-75	297
Underwood, Alexander	33-349	252
Vail, John	35-310	317
Vandewoestyne, Katherine	28-36	49
Varman, Abigail	33-12	222
Varman, Hattil	30-268	163
Wade, Mary	29-357	123

Name	Friend Vol. - Page	Heiss Book Page Number
Walker, Lewis	29-268	111
Walker, William	27-285	31
Walln, Nicholas	28-364	82
Walmsly, Sarah	33-102	232
Walton, Daniel	28-380	85
Walton, William	29-380	126
Wardell, Robert	27-356	41
Watson, William	20-13	90
Webb, Elizabeth	29-77	98
Webster, ·Ann	35-100	301
Webster, Anna	33-84	230
Whartnaby, Elizabeth	29-365	124
Whitewell, Francis	27-124	2
Wickersham, Thomas	29-285	113
Wildman, John	29-413	132
Wiley, Abigail	33-337	251
Wilford, John	28-405	88
Wilkins, Mary	31-53	167
Wilkins, Susanna	29-339	120
Williams, Elinor	31-76	109
Williams, George	30-212	155
Williams, Isaac	29-374	126
Williams, Joanne	29-252	109
Williams, Mary	29-413	131
Willis, Henry	29-308	116
Willis, William	30-12	134
Wills, Elizabeth	31-148	182
Willson, Christopher	30-12	134
Willson, Samuel	33-68	228
Withers, Ralph	28-173	60
Wood, Henry	29-348	80
Wood, John	30-212	155
Wood, Martha	29-348	126
Wood, Thomas	35-84	298

Name	Friend Vol. - Page	Heiss Book Page Number
Woolman, Abner	35-189	307
Woolman, Elizabeth	35-268	314
Woolman, Samuel	31-117	177
Worth, Joseph	29-77	98
Wright, James	32-413	221

Name	Friend Vol. - Page	Heiss Book Page Number
Wright, John	31-67	168
Wyatt, Elizabeth	31-70	170
Wynne, Thomas	27-228	21
Yardley, William	27-243	25

Selected Bibliography

SEE "REFERENCES AND SUGGESTED READING" in each chapter for additional books on specific topics. See the "Quaker Resources—Books, Articles, and Websites" chapter for references to finding aids for specific meetings.

Early Quaker Authors (These works are free online.)

1. Barclay, Robert. *An Apology for the True Christian Divinity,* first published in 1678. Philadelphia: Friends' Book Store, 1908. Barclay (1648–1690) wrote his classic exposition and defense of Quakerism in Latin and published it in 1676 as *Theologiæ Veræ Christianæ Apologia.* He then translated his own book into English. The *Apology* has since been reprinted over 60 times and translated into several other languages. See: http://www.qhpress.org/texts/barclay/apology/index.html.

2. Besse, Joseph. *A collection of the sufferings of the people called Quakers, for the testimony of a good conscience from the time of their being first distinguished by that name in the year 1650 to the time of the act commonly called the Act of toleration granted to Protestant dissenters in the first year of the reign of King William the Third and Queen Mary in the year 1689, 1753 (Vols. 1& 2).* Online at the Digital Quaker Collection, hosted by Earlham College School of Religion. See: http://dqc.esr.earlham.edu or https://archive.org/details/collectionofsuff01bess.

3. Fox, George. Fox produced numerous pamphlets to teach and uplift the Quakers. Over 150 of these pamphlets are online at the Digital Quaker Collection at Earlham College. See: http://dqc.esr.earlham.edu.

4. Pennington, Isaac. *The Works of Isaac Pennington.* An extensive list of titles from four printed volumes. See: http://www.qhpress.org/texts/penington/index.html.

5. Penn, William. *The Journal of William Penn, While Visiting Holland and Germany in 1677.* Penn's firsthand account of his 1677 travels in Holland and Germany visiting Quaker congregations and preaching his message of religious toleration. This is a reprint of the 1879 edition. Britain Yearly Meeting 2006. For other writings by and about Penn, see: http://www.quakerinfo.com/pennbook.shtml.

6. Society of Friends, Philadelphia Yearly Meeting. *A Collection of Memorials Concerning Divers (sic)Deceased Ministers and Others of the People Called Quakers: In Pennsylvania, New Jersey, and Parts Adjacent,*

from Nearly the First Settlement Thereof to the Year 1787: with Some of the Last Expressions and Exhortations of Many of Them. 1787. See: http://tinyurl.com/kpebnuy.

19th-Century Quaker Authors

1. Janney, Samuel. *Memoirs of Samuel Janney.* Philadelphia: Friends' Book Association, 1881

2. Tallack, William. *Friendly Sketches in America.* London: A. W. Bennett, 1861

3. *The Testimony of the Society of Friends on the Continent of America.* Philadelphia: 1830

4. Wilbur, John. *Journal of the Life of John Wilbur, a Minister of the Gospel in the Society of Friends; with Selections from His Correspondence, &c.* Providence, Rhode Island, 1859

20th Century Quaker and non-Quaker Authors

1. Bowden, James. *The History of the Society of Friends in America.* 2 vols. London, 1850, reprinted New York: Arno Press, 1972

2. Brinton, Howard H. *Friends for 300 Years.* 1952. Reprint Wallingford, Pa.: Pendle Hill & Philadelphia Yearly Meeting, 1965 [An excellent history of the Society of Friends.]

3. Cook, Darius B. *Memoirs of Quaker Divide.* Dexter, Iowa: The Dexter Sentinel, 1914

4. Elliott, Errol T. *Quakers on the American Frontier.* Elgin, Illinois: The Brethren Press, 1969

5. Frost, J. William. *The Keithian Controversy in Early Pennsylvania,* Norwood Publications, 1980

6. Hamm, Thomas D. and Willard C. Heiss. *Quaker Genealogies, a Selected List of Books.* Boston: New England Historic Genealogical Society, 1986

7. Hamm, Thomas D. *The Transformation of American Quakerism: Orthodox Friends, 1800–1907.* Bloomington, Indiana: Indiana University Press, 1988

8. Holden, David E. W. *Friends Divided: Conflict and Separation in the Society of Friends.* Richmond, Indiana: Friends United Press, 1988

9. Jones, Rufus M. *The Quakers in the American Colonies.* 1911, reprinted New York: Russell & Russell, 1962

10. Jones, Rufus. *The Later Periods of Quakerism.* 2 volumes. London: Macmillian and Company, 1921

11. Larson, Rebecca. *Daughters of Light: Quaker Women Preaching and Prophesying in the Colonies and Abroad, 1700–1775.* New York: Alfred A. Knopf, 1999

12. Levy, Barry. *Quakers and the American Family: British Settlement in the Delaware Valley.* Oxford University Press, 1992

13. Lippincott, Horace Mather, *Early Philadelphia: Its People, Life and Progress.* Philadelphia: J. B. Lippincott Company, 1917

14. McCracken, George. *Penn's Colony: Genealogical and Historical Materials Relating to the Settlement of Pennsylvania. Volume 2: Welcome Claimants—Proved, Disproved, and Doubtful, with an Account of Some of Their Descendants.* Heritage Books, 2009

15. Milligan, Edward H. and Malcolm J. Thomas. *My Ancestors Were Quakers.* London: Society of Genealogists Enterprises Limited, 2005

16. *Quaker Marriage*, Quaker Tapestry Books, 1994

17. *The Biographical Dictionary of British Quakers in Commerce and Industry 1775–1920.* York: U.K. William Sessions Limited, 2007

18. Nash, Gary. *Quakers and Politics: Pennsylvania, 1680–1726* (Princeton University Press, 1968)

19. Nickalls, John and Fox, George. *The Journal of George Fox: Revised Edition*, Cambridge University Press, 2014

20. Punshon, John. *Portrait in Grey: A Short History of the Quakers.* London: Quaker Home Service, 1984

21. Russell, Elbert. *The History of Quakerism.* New York: Macmillan, 1943

22. Selleck, George A. *Quakers in Boston, 1656–1964: Three Centuries of Friends in Boston and Cambridge.* Cambridge, Mass.: Friends Meeting at Cambridge, 1976

23. Sheppard, Walter Lee, Jr. *Passengers and Ships Prior to 1684. Volume 1 of Penn's Colony: Genealogical and Historical Materials Relating to the Settlement of Pennsylvania.* Heritage Books Reprint, 1996

24. Thomas, Allen C. and Richard H. Thomas. *A History of the Friends in America.* Fifth Edition, Revised and Enlarged by Allen C. Thomas. Philadelphia: John C. Winston Co., 1919

25. Tolles, Frederick B. *Meeting House and Counting House: The Quaker Merchants of Colonial Philadelphia, 1682–1763.* WW Norton & Company, Inc., 1963

26. Trueblood, D. Elton. *The People Called Quakers*, New York: Harper & Row, 1966

27. Weeks, Silas B. and James A. Turrell. *New England Quaker Meetinghouses, Past and Present* Richmond, Indiana: Friends United Press, 2001

28. West, Jessamyn, ed.. *The Quaker Reader,* New York: Viking, 1962. A collection of essays by Fox, Penn, and other notable Quakers.

29. Williams, Walter R. *The Rich Heritage of Quakerism.* Edited reprint with epilogue by Paul Anderson. Newberg, Oregon: The Barclay Press, 1987

Postscript

AS I GATHER MY FINAL thoughts about this book, one issue regarding the Quakers comes to my mind that I feel needs addressing. I am often asked questions, such as: Did all Quakers believe the same way about serving in wars? Did Quakers *always* avoid going to war? As you no doubt realize, in almost all religious denominations there is a spectrum of beliefs from congregation to congregation, and from person to person. This may have been especially true of the Quakers, since they had no authoritative creed or hierarchy. The issue of war was a complicated one for each generation of Quakers.

Colonies each formed their own militia and ostracized those who didn't register. The French & Indian War (1754-1763) was the first organized war effort prior to the Revolutionary War that required Quakers to either serve or defend their faith. Most Friends had strong convictions in terms of their "Peace Testimony". They were opposed to violence of every kind and would not resort to physical force, in order to "set up, pull down, or reorganize any government". They deplored the king's policy toward the colonies, but their dependence was on God; not on man. Their principles were uncompromising; their path straight and narrow; they could do no act either to oppose one party or assist the other. The Philadelphia Yearly Meeting released a statement to the members in 1746, which included the following statements and helps to illustrate their deeply-held principles:

"…it behooves us to show our obedience to the example and precepts of the Prince of Peace, who hath commanded us to love our enemies, and to do good even to them that hate us. Therefore we entreat all that profess themselves members of our Society, to be faithful to that ancient testimony, borne by us ever since we were a people, against bearing arms and fighting; that, by a conduct agreeable to our profession, we may demonstrate ourselves to be real followers of the Messiah, the peaceable Savior, of whose government and peace there shall be no end."

In time, some Quakers felt that they *must* support the Revolution and not allow their neighbors to fight and perhaps die, while they did nothing. They started their own sect called the Free Quakers when they were disowned for their war involvement. Others felt their anti-war convictions so strongly that they left the country altogether, fleeing to Canada. Still others stayed and didn't fight but had double taxes were imposed on them in order to support the war effort; many were incarcerated because they saw it as unfair and refused to pay it.

Some looked for ways to help without compromising their convictions, wanting to help while avoiding disownment for supporting the war. One of my fourth great grandfathers, a Quaker named Isaac Potts, was approached many times to help George Washington's fledgling army. He and his brothers owned several forges and could easily have made musket balls or wheel rims, but they felt strongly that they must refuse. When he was visiting one of his forges, the forge in the valley, the story is told that Isaac overheard George Washington praying the woods nearby, asking for divine help with the war. The General had marched his tired, beaten, sick army to Valley Forge, about 20 miles northwest of British-occupied Philadelphia. His troops were starving

FIGURE F-1: *The Isaac Potts house at Valley Forge was loaned to General Washington during the winter of 1777.*

and cold, sleeping in unheated log cabins with almost no provisions. Other officers had found comfortable lodging at nearby farms, but Washington was determined to stay near his troops.

The story is told that after my grandfather heard the General's lament, he went to his wife and told her that although they pledged not to support the war effort, he felt impressed to lend some sort of support to General Washington. They owned a little home in Valley Forge, so they decided to ask their renter (a cousin) to move out just for the winter. They invited Washington to move in with some of his junior officers, which Washington gratefully did until the end of the winter of 1777-1778. There were 12,000 men encamped at Valley Forge that winter; a quarter of them died before spring arrived. It turned out that no one in the Potts family was disowned for offering lodging to the General. Isaac Potts expressed joy that he could help this good man stating, "I did not know that one could be a military man and a Christian, but I believe this man to be both".

You may have seen a painting called "The Prayer at Valley Forge." It was painted by Arnold Friberg after he learned the story about Isaac Potts and the prayer he overheard.

FIGURE F-2: *The Prayer at Valley Forge.*

Postscript

Throughout the centuries, Quakers have had to make their own decisions about supporting the war. My mother, who grew up as a Quaker in Brooklyn, never let us play with pretend guns as kids. "Lisa", she would say, "thee put down that stick right now!" My father served in World War II, earning his wings as a fighter pilot in the Army Air Corps. He was kept in the states to train others in Texas and did not go overseas to fight. He once confided to me that perhaps it was the earnest prayers of his Quaker wife and parents that kept him stateside. He knew that they were not pleased that he and his brother, ninth-generation Quakers, had enlisted in the war. Disownments were no longer the norm for Quakers in the 1940s; that practice had faded by then. But deeply-held convictions about hurting another person were strong then and remain in hearts today.

Quakers held tightly to their belief that nothing was ever resolved by a show of force and anger. Mahatma Gandhi said it well, "There is no *way* to peace; peace *is* the way".

Index

A

abbreviations in Hinshaw collections, 86–87, 89–90, 93
acknowledgements (apologies), 40
Ancestry.com
  case study, 144–63
  using for Quaker research, 3, 5
anti-slavery efforts, 24–27
apologies (written statements), 40, 76–81

B

baptisms, 40–41
biographies, 181–90
birth registers, 58–60
birthright Friends, 41
Books of Discipline, 44, 76–81, 123–25
burial grounds, 136–37
burial records, 41, 68–71
businesses, 129–31

C

calendars used by Quakers, 41–42, 95–97
California, records for, 106–7
Canada, records for, 103
Certificates of Removal, 13, 42, 72–76
christenings, 40–41
clerks, 43
clothing, 122
conferences, 141–42
convinced Friends, 44

D

dates
  format of, 96–97
  overview, 41
days of the week, 41–42, 97
death records, 68–71
Delaware, records for, 107
Dictionary of Quaker Biography, The, 118
discipline
  apologies, 76–81
  Book of Discipline, 76–81
  Certificates of Removal, 72–75
  disownments, 44, 76–81
disownments, 44, 76–81
double-dating, 96

E

EAQG (*Encyclopedia of American Quaker Geneal-ogy*), 83–84
education, 129
Encyclopedia of American Quaker Genealogy, 83–84, 88–93
England, records for, 104–5

F

FamilySearch.org, using for Quaker research, 4, 7
Fox, George, 11–14
Free Quakers, 45
funerals, 48, 134–35

About the Author

LISA PARRY ARNOLD WAS A birthright member of Westfield Friends Meeting in Cinnaminson, Burlington County, New Jersey. She is a graduate of George School (class of 1971) and Brigham Young University (History/Family History, 2006). She is a Master's degree candidate in history at the University of Nebraska-Kearney. Lisa is a professional genealogist and the Founding President of the Philadelphia Area Chapter of the Association of Professional Genealogists.

Lisa is Senior Content Strategist on the Global Content Team at Ancestry.com, and has been employed there for nine years. Her responsibilities include providing expert research on records and collections including African-American, Native American and church records, among others. She provided research for the *Today Show* and *Good Morning America,* and was part of the research team for NBC's "*Who Do You Think You Are?*" television show.

Lisa is a frequent presenter at national genealogy conferences, and a guest lecturer at the *Institute of Genealogy & Historical Research* (IGHR). She has been a speaker for Ancestry.com at major Ancestry Day events held in numerous cities around the United States. In addition to being a lecturer and author, Lisa teaches family history classes in her community. She is former Director of the Family History Center in Valley Forge, Pennsylvania.

Lisa's interest in genealogy stems from her heritage as a Quaker. Her family lines extend back to the early Quakers, who were followers of George Fox in England and came to the colonies in the days of William Penn. Like the ten generations before her, Lisa was raised in the Quaker religion. She attended Quaker schools, and was married in a Quaker wedding ceremony in the Westfield Friends Meetinghouse in 1974. She completed an internship at Swarthmore College in 2003, working with the largest Quaker record collection in America, housed at the Swarthmore Friends Historical Library. It was the internship at Swarthmore that led to the writing of this book.

Made in the USA
San Bernardino, CA
02 August 2014